Being a Presence for Students

TEACHING AS A LIVED DEFENSE OF LIBERAL EDUCATION

Jeff Frank

LEVER
PRESS

Copyright © 2019 by Jeffery Frank

Lever Press (leverpress.org) is a publisher of pathbreaking scholarship. Supported by a consortium of liberal arts institutions focused on, and renowned for, excellence in both research and teaching, our press is grounded on three essential commitments: to be a digitally native press, to be a peer-reviewed, open access press that charges no fees to either authors or their institutions, and to be a press aligned with the ethos and mission of liberal arts colleges.

This work is licensed under the Creative Commons Attribution- NoDerivatives 4.0 International License. To view a copy of this license, visit http://creativecommons.org/licenses/by-nd/4.0/ or send a letter to Creative Commons, PO Box 1866, Mountain View, CA 94042, USA.

The complete manuscript of this work was subjected to a partly closed ("single blind") review process. For more information, please see our Peer Review Commitments and Guidelines at https://www.leverpress.org/peerreview

DOI: https://doi.org/10.3998/mpub.11567473
Print ISBN: 978-1-64315-007-9
Open access ISBN: 978-1-64315-008-6

Library of Congress Control Number: 2019944548

Published in the United States of America by Lever Press, in partnership with Amherst College Press and Michigan Publishing

Contents

Acknowledgments

This work would not have been possible without the generous support of the John William Miller Fellowship. I especially want to thank Michael McGandy for his attentiveness and passion for Miller's philosophy. I am grateful for his feedback on the project, though the views expressed in this book are my own.

I am also grateful to St. Lawrence University for providing me with sabbatical. Thank you also to Karl Schonberg and Alison Del Rossi for taking over leadership of the education department. Your leadership made this work possible, and your lived defense of liberal education is one I aspire to.

The librarians at Williams College were extremely generous with their time and expertise. Thank you especially to Anne Peale, Lisa Conathan, and Sylvia Kennick-Brown.

Thank you also to everyone at Lever Press, especially Beth Bouloukos and Amanda Karby. The outside readers were extremely generous with their feedback and suggestions, and I hope they see the imprint of their work in this project.

Finally, thank you to liberal educators. I was transformed by my liberal education at Middlebury College, and I value the continuing guidance and friendship of Dan Brayton. He took the time and care to show me what was possible, and I hope to be the educator and mentor to my students that he was to me.

Member Institution Acknowledgments

Lever Press is a joint venture. This work was made possible by the generous support of Lever Press member libraries from the following institutions:

Adrian College
Agnes Scott College
Allegheny College
Amherst College
Bard College
Berea College
Bowdoin College
Carleton College
Claremont Graduate University
Claremont McKenna College
Clark Atlanta University
Coe College
College of Saint Benedict / Saint John's University
The College of Wooster
Denison University
DePauw University
Earlham College
Furman University
Grinnell College
Hamilton College
Harvey Mudd College
Haverford College
Hollins University
Keck Graduate Institute
Kenyon College
Knox College
Lafayette College Library
Lake Forest College
Macalester College
Middlebury College
Morehouse College
Oberlin College

Pitzer College
Pomona College
Rollins College
Santa Clara University
Scripps College
Sewanee: The University of the South
Skidmore College
Smith College
Spelman College
St. Lawrence University
St. Olaf College
Susquehanna University
Swarthmore College
Trinity University
Union College
University of Puget Sound
Ursinus College
Vassar College
Washington and Lee University
Whitman College
Willamette University
Williams College

PROLOGUE

JOHN WILLIAM MILLER'S LIVED DEFENSE OF LIBERAL EDUCATION

In the winter of 2017, after learning I got tenure at St. Lawrence University, I also learned that Stanley Bates, my undergraduate mentor at Middlebury College, had died. The process of getting tenure made me more reflective than normal about why teaching at a liberal arts college mattered, but the death of Bates forced me to consider what it meant to be a devoted educator with an urgency I wasn't prepared for. I wouldn't be living the life I was if I had not met Professor Bates my first semester in college. He had a profound impact on me, helping me become the person I am now. I had never pressed myself to explain his impact, but as a way of expressing my gratitude for what Bates did for me, I felt as if I needed to move beyond vague appreciation and do something more significant.

How is it that a professor can impact a student in the ways Stanley Bates impacted me? I don't find myself drawing on things he said on a regular basis, but I often recall sitting in his office and feeling like I was in the presence of something important. I draw on that feeling regularly. Though this was never made explicit, he clearly communicated that there was something serious in me I could get in touch with, and that there was something serious in the books and ideas we were studying together that would emerge if I dedicated myself to them. Being in his presence taught me that the deep desire I brought to college, the desire to find something meaningful to devote myself to, could kindle into something more as I took myself and my studies more seriously.

I credit this moral seriousness, in part, as the heart of teaching at a liberal arts college. I teach because I believe that a liberal education can be transformative. A young person full of longing and confusion can read a book or engage in a discussion or write a paper and this can then empower them with the confidence it takes to undertake risky and difficult work in the future. As I wrote my tenure documents, I was filled with a spirit of gratitude that I got to take part in this process. I was grateful that I was joined with professors like Bates in the work of helping young people move from confusion and a desire for a self they only have an intimation of to empowerment and a sense of agency, without ever explicitly telling them who they should be or what they should think. The liberal arts professor who acts with moral seriousness doesn't want a student to become something already existing—a liberal, a conservative, fit for a profession. What a professor wants for a student is for them to understand, through the seriousness they experience at college, that their calling is often far more difficult than that. Oftentimes the options we are presented with are not good enough, and we have to envision or create alternatives. Our education gives us the morale to take on that difficult work.

To put the point another way, a liberal education is an education in skepticism and commitment. A liberal education causes a student to ask questions and to see the flaws in even the most well-argued or earnestly held position. But this education is not merely critical. Students graduating from liberal arts colleges also desire a life of commitment. An effective liberal education allows a student to combine deep skepticism with an appreciation for the good in its many forms and a willingness to commit to conserving what is good and create conditions for flourishing. I feel that I learned this lesson from my education at Middlebury, but I cannot point to any single course or event that taught me this lesson directly. Rather, and on reflection, it was something about feeling the living presence of liberal education through its trustees that educated me.

It may be a strange way of putting it, but I saw Bates as a representative of a world that I thought was good and worthy of my aspiration.[1] There were other professors like this as well. Dan Brayton taught and lived in a way that immediately demonstrated the good of being liberally educated. Like many professors at liberal arts colleges, when I was in Brayton's office, I was listened to and cared about in a way that I never experienced in my life up to that point. Though I saw the limitations of my thinking quite clearly, I also felt capable of an expansiveness of thought while sitting there in the presence of someone who experienced that expansiveness and wanted me to as well. When I think about my own work as a professor, I see how important it is that I try to be fully present when I am with my students in the classroom or during office hours. I am coming to think that the best defense of liberal education that we can offer is a lived one. Through our teaching and our very presence with students, we can enact and embody the ideals of rigorous questioning and skepticism combined with a devotion to those things we care deeply about.

When liberal education is under attack, as it is now, it is very tempting to move away from this type of lived defense and on to something that is better described as defensiveness. By defensiveness I mean moving away from thinking about the unique goods internal to liberal education and offering external justifications. There are good strategic reasons to highlight the instrumental outcomes of a liberal arts education,[2] just as it is good to show the ways that a liberal education can prepare young people for democractic citizenship.[3] But as important as these defenses tend to be, they also seem to fall flat when we need them most: when we are standing in a front of a group of college students. Though the external defense may convince a student and their parents to choose a liberal arts college, it is how they experience the presence of liberal education that will ultimately convince them of its good.

§

It would've been much easier if Bates had written his philosophy of education or if he was what critics of liberal education claim professors are: partisans who tell students what to think. Neither were true. But he did something else. He empowered me to take up the work of developing a philosophy of teaching at a liberal arts college. I feel the best way I can show my gratitude for what I learned at Middlebury, and the teaching I get to do now at St. Lawrence, is to create ways of defending the liberal arts internally, helping professors at liberal arts colleges communicate, through their presence in the classroom and with students, that liberal education matters. In this book, I turn to John William Miller (1895–1978), a longtime philosophy professor at Williams College (1924–1960), to create this philosophy of teaching at a liberal arts institution, and I want to take a moment to explain this choice.

When you read about Miller, one thing becomes immediately apparent: he was a presence at Williams.[4] Importantly, he was not a teacher who tried to be popular with students or who was looking to win converts through charismatic pedagogy. His commitment to the importance of philosophy struck a chord with his students; he didn't need pedagogical tricks to convince them of the importance of liberal education. He lived its importance. But Miller published very little during his life, and we owe it to his students that his work has found its way into print. At the end of his life, students began the process of publishing his work with W. W. Norton & Company, and eventually five books and an anthology were published. This strikes me as one of the most moving testaments to Miller's importance. His students thought there was something so significant about what he taught through his presence in the classroom that they wanted to find some way of replicating this and sharing it with those who didn't have the experience of studying with him.

In addition to the volumes of Miller's work that have been published with the help of his students,[5] several studies of Miller's work highlight the significance of his philosophy and make the strong case for why we should take his philosophy seriously today.[6] I find value in Miller's philosophy and the published commentary on it, but I aim to do something different in this small book. When I think about Miller I think about teaching, and my hope—when I began studying Miller—was that something in his unpublished writings housed at Williams College would give me the language to talk about teaching at a liberal arts college.[7]

Happily, I found that there is a lot that we can learn about teaching at a liberal arts college from studying Miller. In particular, Miller focuses on two elements of teaching and liberal education that tend to be ignored: presence and morale. For Miller, liberal education is less about a curriculum and more about a way of being with students. A teacher must take seriously his or her *presence* in the classroom and they must also see their purpose as helping build a student's *morale*. What is striking about this way of thinking about liberal education is that it doesn't look outside of the classroom for a justification of this form of educating. Rather, liberal education, in Miller's view, is defended each day by the way it is lived and enacted in the classroom.

§

Though Miller will be at the heart of this book in many ways, I don't see this book as a scholarly study of him.[8] Rather, I take Miller as exemplary of someone who sees himself as a trustee of liberal education. I turn to Miller both because of his status as a teacher and because he is able to articulate a lived defense of liberal education in a way that I have not yet experienced in my reading life.[9] I note this because I want readers to have in mind their versions of professors like Bates and Brayton as they read. Though I was fortunate enough to attend a small liberal arts college and to teach at one now, and though the exemplary professors I turn to are white men, I don't mean for my account to be exclusionary. It is important to stress this point. As I hope will be clear as the book progresses, I don't believe liberal education is reliant on a closed canon, and I think trustees of liberal education are made up of a wide range of people from a variety of social, economic, sexual, and political backgrounds. I speak from my lived experience, but what is yours? Even if you did not attend, or do not teach at, a liberal arts college, you may have experienced liberal education or provide a liberal education to students. More, as you read, I ask that you envision the professors who freed you to experience personal transformation because of their teaching and their presence. Having their work in mind will help you engage with the process of developing your own lived defense of liberal education.

§

The book is organized as follows. The next chapter will offer a discussion of central ideas from Miller's philosophy of teaching and liberal education: morale and presence. With this background in place, Miller's previously unpublished 1943 notes "Reflections on the Liberal Education" will be presented in full. The chapter following these notes will be an extended commentary. As with the rest of the book, the goal of this extended commentary is not primarily meant to be a contribution to scholarship on Miller or even the extensive and always growing literature on liberal education. Rather, it is meant to help readers think about teaching at institutions committed to liberal education and how we can offer our students a lived defense of liberal education. The concluding chapter presents ways a professor can think about how to develop presence and morale in their own classroom. It won't offer "tips and tricks," but it will give professors an opportunity to consider how they might improve their practice.

The tone of this book is meant to be invitational, and it won't assume a background in Miller, the literature on liberal education, or a background in philosophy and education. Instead, the goal is to help those of us who care about liberal education find ways to think about how we might support it more fully. For those of us who are teachers at liberal arts colleges or in programs committed to liberal education, I hope this book helps us become more present with our students, so that we might more fully live the ways we value liberal education.

CHAPTER ONE

INTRODUCTION: PRESENCE AND MORALE

In 1952, John William Miller delivered the Phi Beta Kappa address during Hobart College's commencement. This lecture, "The Scholar as Man of the World," offers an excellent statement of his philosophy of education. It covers a lot of ground, and in this chapter I focus on one of the stated aims of the lecture: exploring the importance of morale for college students. Toward the middle of his talk, Miller makes this point very directly, stating: "For it is a grievous thing to see the young student depart [college] without those convictions on which his morale depends."[10]

It is worth considering why, of all the things Miller could bring to Hobart from his experience as a professor at Williams College, he chose morale. Instead of rehashing platitudes about liberal education—congratulating Phi Beta Kappans for their hard work, for being campus leaders, for being models of the well-rounded individual—Miller's speech eschewed the superficial and raised the philosophical and educational significance of the state of morale at liberal arts colleges.[11] In asking these deeper questions about morale, Miller was reanimating a concern addressed by Ralph Waldo Emerson.

In 1837, one hundred and fifteen years earlier, Emerson delivered the most famous Phi Beta Kappa address, "The American Scholar."[12] In that speech to Harvard students, Emerson lamented the state of higher education in America. Still bound to European models and imitative in nature, Emerson hoped to free young Americans from this past, empowering them to be thinkers, unafraid of where their thought might take them. Emerson hoped to inspire thinkers who would be active: transforming work into vocation and living into an art. The American scholar would be no bookworm; they would use thought to transform this country into the ideals expressed in its founding documents. Miller was a great admirer of Emerson, and it makes sense that he would use the occasion to build off of key ideas from "The American Scholar."[13]

Emerson wanted his audience of students to see that old ways of thinking would not fit the here-and-now conditions of their present experience, and he urged them to risk creating something new. The risk is real, because breaking with tradition threatens to leave us with no foundation at all. If we turn our back on models that are not yet broken for the promise of possibility, who is to say that what we come up with will not be worse than what we have now? Miller, drawing on Emerson, was reminding his audience that the well-worn clichés we repeat at liberal arts institutions could become deadening. Instead of giving us the strength and courage it will take to face the future, we take refuge in the known. This is problematic, for Miller, because it cuts us off from the necessity of self-criticism. Instead of offering an honest reckoning with the world and our place in it, we can hide within the emptiness of a form. We retreat into the title—I am a Phi Beta Kappa, I am the graduate of a liberal arts institution—but we don't take the risk of thought that these titles are meant to signify. A student needs to have the courage to take the risk of thinking, and Miller's address is about testing whether or not liberal education is capable of generating this type of *morale* in students. By morale, I see Miller getting at the idea that liberal education should empower students to balance self-criticism and commitment. We need to risk breaking with the old through the exercise of self-criticism but must also trust that this self-criticism will not leave us completely adrift. Rather, self-criticism is the foundation for mature commitment and engagement with a world of value.

We can see this point more clearly when we appreciate that Miller wrote his dissertation under the direction of William Ernest Hocking, a philosopher who wrote insightfully about morale in American society. Hocking contrasts superficial morale with mature morale in a 1941 essay that offers a key to understanding Miller's thinking.[14] Superficial morale can be understood as the type of morale favored by dictators. This type of morale is unthinking; using fear and magical thinking, the dictator stirs up energy and maintains it with threats, intimidation, and lies.[15] This type of morale often disappears when subjected to honest criticism, hence the dictator's need to keep people from exercising thought. By contrast, mature morale is self-chosen and survives when it is subjected to self-criticism. Though the proponents of superficial morale correctly appreciate that commitment and passion are dispelled when people are allowed to think and question their values, mature morale is built on a different understanding of the type of education needed to maintain morale. Mature morale is cultivated by freely taking on commitments and sticking with them when faced with external and internal challenges. It is a loyalty that embraces self-criticism and the effort needed to sustain value. Here is how Hocking describes it:

> If there is anything free about the human being, it is to be found here, in this deed of gift. It is the surplus push put behind performance to give it a certain "go," so that not every accident or obstacle will bring a halt; it is an original drive, not a borrowed or imitative spurt, arising from one's own conviction and good will.[16]

We are free to put forward our best effort as a "deed of gift." Though superficial morale is often coerced by external rewards or threats, mature morale is built on conviction and good will. This was the morale that Miller hoped to see in graduates of institutions committed to liberal education. Once the promise of rewards is gone—no Phi Beta Kappa to achieve, for example—will graduates practice the freedom of giving their best effort based on their convictions and good will? Or, will they fall prey to forms of superficial morale and the lack of self-criticism that comes with it? What Miller advocates is the difficult balance between conviction and criticism.[17]

§

Miller's thinking on morale remains important. We live in a time when there is a risk that even our best students will lose motivation when they leave behind the scaffolding of credentials that college offers. We also live in a time when cynicism and hopelessness is palpable. The individual feels small in the face of climate change, income inequality, and antidemocratic movements across the globe. On top of this, we've taken on the role of promoting critical thinkers exceedingly well, and this can leave students demoralized. They may have come into college with a set of political and religious beliefs that offer and sustain meaning and purpose, but by graduation they may be left with more questions than convictions.[18] The balance between conviction and criticism is off, and students are unable to activate a mature sense of morale. This is a problem that we should all be concerned with, as Miller was when he addressed Hobart graduates.

Before further considering Miller's approach to morale and its development, it is worthwhile to pause and consider that some professors may find the very idea of developing student morale overstepping the academic mission of a college. A professor listening to Miller's address may hope for more of a focus on what the liberal arts, as an academic curriculum, can do for the intellectual lives of students. Though some readers may share this belief, that liberal education should stick to academic matters only, it is hard for me to share this narrow academic focus given what I experienced at a liberal arts college and what I know about why these schools were founded.[19] Even when a liberal arts college wasn't explicitly founded on religious grounds, these colleges were deeply concerned with educating the young to become people of character. And, as many of these schools grew away from their religious foundations, the goal of character development remained important.[20] As such, it seems central that liberal education remains connected to the mission of cultivating a student's character, without becoming dogmatic or moralistic. In a note written toward the end of his life, Miller spoke to this point in the following way: "Philosophy does no one a service. It furthers no purposes. Its business is morale. It is not morals. I was no moralist."[21] Miller is no moralist; he doesn't have any predetermined end he is pointing students toward, be it a career, a viewpoint, or a political belief. Rather, allowing students to really struggle with a text, an idea, or a belief that they feel is unshakeable can activate their morale, giving them a new sense of power. Though criticism can feel merely destructive, it can also help students discover their power to make sense of the world for themselves.

Here, again, I am reminded of Emerson's thinking in "The American Scholar." When colleges idolize books and positions developed by leading thinkers, inscribing the names of authors into the sides of libraries as if they were meant to be worshipped, they keep students from appreciating that all of these books were written by men and women who were once young people themselves. Emerson wants to remind professors and students of this fact.[22] Instead of training young people to read the "right" books or hold the "right" ideas, college can educate young people to feel the sense of morale one needs to take ownership of one's own thinking and writing. Miller is getting at this point in the brief passage quoted above. The purpose of philosophical study is not to lead students to a predetermined end but to empower them to be mindful of how beliefs are formed and held. It is not about teaching morals; it is about showing students what it means to balance self-criticism and conviction so that one can experience a sense of morale. For Miller, like Emerson, college is not about getting students to think a certain way, conforming to a predetermined position. Rather, education does no one a service: it invites them to determine what is worth devotion, and learn what it means to care for what one finds, on reflection, to be worthy of one's care.[23]

Where Miller and Emerson part company is Miller's focus on what he calls "local control." Emerson's strength lies in provoking readers to shake off traditional ways of thinking that don't have the power to generate mature morale. But this strength can often turn into a weakness, when a reader of Emerson becomes critical of anything but an ideal of perfection that one never experiences in daily living. Though Emerson categorized his philosophy as one that is in touch with the ordinary,[24] his faith that exercising self-criticism through the practice of nonconformity would naturally bring us into concert with others who are willing to practice nonconformity seems unrealistic. Emerson's world is one notable for its lack of strife.[25] According to Emerson, once we turn our backs on conformity we open ourselves up to a sustaining connection with the divine that ensures us that we are connected to all others, because they too share that connection to the divine, no matter how dimly they apprehend the connection. In Emerson, the person who practices self-criticism and nonconformity will find their community.

What is particularly troubling about this aspect of Emerson's thinking is that it neglects the importance of conserving the world of ordinary, actually existing objects. When we are divinely assured of our values and the cooperation of a community to sustain those values, we may lose the morale necessary to actually maintain those values. Because Miller doesn't share Emerson's divine assurance policy, he argues the necessity of taking responsibility for being stewards of what we value in our daily lives, knowing full well that this may put us at odds with others.[26] Instead of finding a community committed to what we care about when we practice nonconformity, our convictions can lead us to conflicts in the local contexts of our everyday life.

Miller calls us back to the things of this world. Instead of giving students visions of the divine, the ahistorical, and the ideal, Miller calls them back to the contingent and the mundane. Here is how he puts it in his Hobart address:

> We control only local situations, and not the universe as a whole. . . . Existential knowledge, born of restraint, furnishes the sole avenue to such actual, if limited, power as we possess, or can come to possess.[27]

Existential knowledge is a key term Miller uses several times in his address, and what he means by it is the type of knowledge that a student earns by making the attempt to balance criticism and stewardship in the local context of their daily living. When a college student makes an argument about something that is disconnected from their experience of the world, they don't feel the same restraint they would if they were arguing about, for example, issues that exist on their campus. For example, if the student wrote a paper about systemic racism, they may learn a good deal from the experience, but they might not experience existential knowledge. Existential knowledge is more likely to arise if they wrote about the ways their campus exhibits systemic racism in its policies and practices. When we practice criticism of something near to us, in a spirt of maintaining what is good about the practice while excising what doesn't stand up to critical inquiry, we are positioned to feel the limited power we possess or can come to possess.

The work of thinking in a college classroom can become so divorced from local situations and actual restraints that students leaving the bubbles of their college campuses may be unprepared for a world that doesn't respond to their thought with the same interest they experienced as undergraduates. When this occurs, students can quickly become demoralized, doubting the efficacy of their college educations, and, by extension, the practical power of thought itself. Miller sees this as a real threat, one made worse by what he sees as excesses of progressive education. For Miller, constraint and conflict are inevitable; contra some strains of progressive education, a student cannot simply follow their interests and passions and find a welcoming community. A learner needs to experience the restraint of local conditions and to feel counter interests and counter passions in order to develop a sense of morale. Importantly, Miller makes it very clear that the Emersonian drive, followed by many progressive educators, from individual interest to welcoming community, is deeply flawed. We are limited in our powers, in large part, because conflict is a reality. Instead of feeling as if our power is unlimited, we should seek to test the limits of our power in local situations. Instead of arguing the merits of a position abstractly and to a receptive audience, something that seems increasingly encouraged as the possibilities for nonembodied discussion flower online,[28] it is imperative that students take the risk of demonstrating the good of that same position to a fellow student or a family member who may not, at least initially, see its good. This is experiencing existential education. The student would feel the success or failure of their current power to critically sustain values in the here and now of our shared world.

The important thing is trading a world free from conflict for a world of constraint. It is only when we stand behind our values in the face of opposition that we learn about our commitment to those values. If we readily give in to opposition, if we cannot draw on a deep well of morale to assert the good of what we value, we learn something very important. Unless we are willing to live our values, to act on their behalf, it is hard to say that we actually hold the value we assert. I don't want to give the impression that holding a value is necessarily adversarial. But it does involve a commitment that is often limiting. We cannot value everything, because to value something means to devote time, a terribly limited resource, to promoting and practicing what we value. Miller makes the point this way: "To act is to see oneself as limited, and as a trustee of value."[29] When I act, say, by assigning one book and not another, one assignment and not another, I am limiting myself. But though I've limited myself to teaching one book, I am also holding the book up as something of value. By teaching it, I act as a trustee of its value.

To return to a point made earlier, I think we often mistake critical thinking as the sole goal of a liberal education. There is no doubt that we must learn how to be critical thinkers, but critical thinking should not destroy the possibility of being a trustee of value. For example, an education in critical thinking can help me see the flaws in something I value very deeply. But seeing the flaw in something should not be an excuse for discarding it in the hopes that I will find something beyond reproach. Rather, a liberal education can show us what it might mean to devote ourselves to imperfect things. Even though I may understand the ways that, for example, a composer may be, all things considered, a better composer than the one I love, this gives me no reason to not love them and devote myself to their music to the relative neglect of the other composer. Learning how to balance criticism and devotion is an important art that should be cultivated through liberal education. More controversially, we should also help a student see the flaws of a political party without sending the message that they cannot commit to that party. And, just like the composer example above, we can see that a preference or commitment to one party should not imply that the other is evil, stupid, or not worthy of the devotion that other people show it. Obviously, there are some ideas and positions that are indeed evil and unreasonable and should be called such on college campuses and in civil discourse, but there are far more things that are worthy of our respect and devotion. The trick is helping a student find those things that they can commit to even while acknowledging their imperfections and limitations.

To be a trustee of value is to be someone filled with this type of mature morale. Given my limited time, I cannot care about everything—though I can respect the things that other people devote their care to—and given the good of critical thinking, I can see the flaws of the things I am committed to. I also realize that the things I care about can very easily go away, either through direct attack or simply, though no less damaging, through lack of care and attention. Here, I often think of local historical societies. Sometimes the existence of these organizations is directly attacked, say, when funding cuts are made. More often than not they are put at risk through lack of care. No one is willing to devote the time it takes to make these societies exist. There are many similar things we can imagine. If we stop caring about certain authors or certain ideas, they won't be available to future generations in the ways they would if we stood as their passionate representative: a trustee of their value.[30]

As Miller addresses Hobart graduates and, by extension, graduates of other liberal arts colleges, he is asking them to become trustees of value. Not abstractly but locally. Their education has empowered them to look critically at objects of their care, which is needed. They must also continue to care about those things they find valuable, even as they continue to subject them to critical scrutiny. For example, I consider myself a devotee of liberal education. This does not mean I find this form of education beyond reproach. Discourses at liberal arts colleges can become exclusionary, or unduly partisan; liberal arts institutions can be unsafe spaces for students, they can become bastions of elitism and toxic masculinity. Noting these very real problems with liberal education doesn't mean abandoning my devotion; it means drawing on morale to address the problems and issues that emerge through my critical care. To defend an imperfect thing open to its many flaws doesn't bring the same feelings of righteousness as when someone feels they are defending the one true path. But this mature morale is sustaining and brings with it unique feelings of tenderness for the very imperfect thing one hopes to sustain through one's devotion. Graduates of liberal arts colleges need that combination of the critical spirit and the willing devotion to the good. Miller beautifully expresses this to graduates of Hobart, and the message remains an important one today.

§

An important question remains: How is morale taught, or how can it be fostered? One suggestion is already offered in the form of existential education. Students need to feel what it is like to exert local control, testing their growing power in situations where there are actual, not just hypothetical, stakes. Even as a student, I was bothered by the use of thought experiments in philosophy. They didn't seem meaningful, and they also struck me as bizarrely mean-spirited. Many involved deciding who lived and who died: kill a good friend (or a child or a husband) or a scientist who would cure cancer. Save the drowning person, though the risk of your own death is high (now, what if the person was your child, or that scientist), and so on. These types of experiments did incite thought, and I don't want to negate the experiences of others who find them meaningful. But they never felt real to me. What was real to me, when I was in college, were questions like: How can I be a good son? My parents are making very real sacrifices to send me to college, and they want me to continue going to church. But the education they are providing me is making me see the limitations of the faith I grew up in. Would it be wrong if I experimented with other faiths? Or, some men on the team I am a part of say extraordinarily sexist and misogynist things. What should I do in this situation? What is the best answer? Quitting, confronting the men, or ignoring it and studying the patriarchy in college so that I might know how to act in the future?[31] Thinking about who should die in a lifeboat did nothing to help me answer those questions.[32]

To help a student experience existential learning, philosophy, and the humanities more generally they should become more Socratic in the way Miller understood Socrates. Socrates was not peddling a method,[33] he was speaking to people at a point of their real need, and helping them discover, through discussion, what action they should undertake. Part of a liberal education is preparing students for the work of discovering what ideas they are willing to stand behind, so that they are prepared to commit to taking an action, knowing, as discussed above, that by acting they are leaving the universal and accepting limitation.

What this will look like will vary across campus context and discipline, but it is worth thinking through how we can give students the experience of balancing criticism with commitment. One way to do this is to assign things like reflective journals or response papers, where students are given opportunities to develop what they think and what a reading, or a piece of art, or a scientific experiment means to the way they will approach living. The goal of assignments like these is to help students become critical and reflective. Breaking the habit of discerning what a teacher wants and trying to provide the "right" answer, students begin to take seriously what it means to hold a belief and the consequences of failing to reflect on beliefs that guide action and policy making.[34] Students want to be impacted by their education, especially students who very consciously choose a liberal arts college. They want to live more wisely, they want to make a positive difference in the world, and they expect professors to help them do it. They are not looking for a guru or someone to show them "the way."[35] They want to be put in conversation with books and ideas that speak to their real need, and then be given opportunities to develop their thinking around that need.

The care with which we listen to a student during office hours or the care we devote to providing feedback on things like their reflective journals will help them experience existential learning in a powerful way. We show them that they need to cultivate their moral sense so that they can exert positive agency in the world. If we thought for them or didn't allow them to feel the burden of exercising thought, they wouldn't be in a position to develop the morale they need to face challenges in the future.

In addition to facilitating existential learning, we also stand as representatives of liberal education. Teaching is an unavoidably moral act, and this is nowhere truer than at a small liberal arts college.[36] Our students come to college hoping to grow as people, and they look to us as examples of people who are trying to do that as well. They shouldn't expect answers from us (let alone *the* answer), but they do want to know that we are the type of person who can demonstrate the good, are the living proof, of the education they are undertaking.

I think this may be hard for some professors to accept, especially given how difficult the job market in academia is, the careerism taught in many graduate schools, and the fear that being a moral presence will mean politicizing the classroom. These are very different points, but they all contribute to making a teacher less of a *presence* in their classroom and college community. Take the first two points. The job market is hard, so if the only job you are offered is at a liberal arts college, you are likely to accept it, even though you may not fully appreciate what these schools mean to students and alumni. Or, even if you understand the mission of a liberal arts college, the careerist voice will often encourage movement and not commitment. Why stay at a liberal arts school when you can make a larger impact at a big research-intensive university? The third point, the fear of politicizing the classroom, can make a professor overly cautious and this cautiousness can make it seem as if they aren't fully present in the classroom. The risk for professors in our highly polarized times is very real, as cable news channels and websites look for examples of "tenured radicals" indoctrinating youth, but our students deserve professors who take the risk of living their commitments to liberal education by offering a lived defense of this education. This doesn't mean politicizing the classroom; it means being present as a trustee of the value of liberal education. It means modeling the morale that balances criticism with commitment.

A teacher's presence is a manifestation of their morale. This is a key, if complicated, component of Miller's philosophy of education. Someone with morale risks the necessary limitations of taking action. They commit to something fully, even in the face of the flaws and limitations of what they are committed to. For Miller, this willingness to commit also issues forth in a presence. The person who lives their commitments has a presence. To go back to the example of the local history museum, the person who commits to preserving local history, in the face of budget cuts and general neglect of their work, has a presence that can be felt when someone visits a local museum or works to uncover a piece of local history. The local historian persists in their work in the face of obstacles and without promise of reward, and this persistence gives them presence. Though they could choose easier things to devote themselves to, they follow their passion and live their commitment: this makes them a presence. At the risk of going on too long at this point, I think of my daughter's fiddle teacher when I think about presence as well. My daughter's fiddle teacher sees herself as responsible for passing down the songs that were passed down to her, and her care for the traditions of fiddle music is immediately felt. And, this presence is deeply educative. This teacher doesn't have to tell my daughter explicitly, "this music matters, so you must practice"; the teacher's devotion to the music makes my daughter feel its importance. The teacher offers a lived defense of fiddle music and this is felt by her students in her very presence.

Turning to the professor at a liberal arts college, I think it is important that we appreciate the importance of this type of presence and work to develop it. Philosopher of education Cristina Cammarano has written very insightfully on presence in teaching, making the case that a teacher's presence is central to her effectiveness as a teacher.[37] A teacher who doesn't have a presence in the classroom cannot build trust and connection with students, whereas a teacher with presence can get students to develop self-trust and take the risks necessary to develop their own morale. For a college professor to have presence in the classroom, they must live their commitment to students and the subject matter by being present in the local conditions of the classroom. The professor is not teaching anywhere or anyone: they are teaching these students in this classroom at this point in their intellectual, social, emotional, and moral development (and at this particular historical and political moment). The professor must live in this space and yet still stand as a representative of where students are not yet. Students are just beginning to learn the material and who they are as thinkers and actors in the world; the professor is farther along in this journey.

Professors often make the mistake of wishing the impossible: that they were teaching some ideal student in some ideal setting. Miller reminds us that we act under local constraints. If we want to persist as a professor at the liberal arts college where we find ourselves, we have to learn how to develop a presence in that place by committing to becoming a trustee of what is valuable in that place and with those particular students who are given to us.

Here I want to turn to some things Miller says directly about presence and its cultivation. The first is a very interesting remark provoked by Miller's student who claims that it is frustrating when a teacher doesn't get out of the way and let the author speak for her or himself. Miller argues that, especially in the humanities, a teacher cannot help but be present when teaching. There is no way to impersonally present a poem, as Miller writes:

> A teacher of poetry not *now* moved by the poem, not presenting its force in his own words, has not shown what was ever alive in the poem itself. But this is a peculiarity of *all* humanities. They cannot be "taught," as geometry can be taught, the teacher never appearing in what he says.[38]

If we want a student to engage with poetry, for example, we must be present with the poem and present the poem to our students in a way that makes it come alive. Going through the motions of teaching does not make the aliveness of what we are teaching manifest for our students. Here I am reminded of those teachers who present the same PowerPoint presentations each semester and then wonder why students don't find the topics interesting. For Miller, teaching is something like a sacramental act. The professor must be present in the classroom if the students are to feel the force of what is taught.[39] They must be ready to be surprised anew by the insight of the poem or the power of the poem to move students. It is good to appreciate what this feels like when we are teaching, the moments when we feel fully alive to our students and what we are teaching. These are the moments we should rely on when planning instruction and thinking about the qualities of good teaching. If the teacher is not moved by what is taught, if they cannot feel its force, then it is hard to know how the students will develop an interest in, let alone a passion for, the material.

Being present in the classroom does not mean being the center of the classroom in an egoistic way. As Cammarano helpfully reminds us, "Big egos take up too much room, shrinking the possibilities for the presence of others—without which no presence is possible. Presence is receptive, attentive, open."[40] In a letter written to a former student wondering how he can become a stronger professor, Miller offers some very good advice when he writes:

> Let your own appreciation of a man appear more obvious than your appraisal or criticism. Nobody will miss seeing your mind in so far as you exhibit understanding of others.... For the most part it is the common world—not yours or mine—that needs to be exhibited. As I say, nobody will miss finding out about your own mind if it shows itself in the effort to make the other attractive.[41]

I am tempted to let this stand on its own without comment, because it is wonderfully delivered. When Miller suggests that a teacher cannot help but appear in their teaching of a poem, he is very clearly not urging teachers to make their opinions known to their students—just the opposite. I love the way he puts it to his former student. A professor does not need to judge and rank and criticize. A professor's appreciation goes much farther in establishing an educative presence in the classroom than a merely critical attitude.

Though critical thinking is an incontrovertible end of a liberal education, we should not neglect the importance of appreciative understanding, something that can be even harder to learn.[42] For example, I do not think I am alone in feeling that criticism is a very easy mode for me as a professor. Given something to read, I can very easily find ways in which it can be improved. But tell me to explain why I love and admire something and tell me that I have to do so in an intellectually sophisticated way—that is much harder. According to Miller, a professor should be moved each day they teach by what is being taught. More, the appreciative attention that they bring to bear on the material teaches students what it means to be a trustee of value. Morale and presence are inextricably linked. Though criticism may give a teacher an immediate sense of power, I think Miller is right in the advice he gives his former student about teaching. Nobody will miss hearing your knockdown arguments against something, but a student's passion might be sparked if you do the work of explaining why something is worthy of their care and attention. A teacher's presence is established anew in each act of appreciation, each act of teaching students why they should take an interest and care about learning to be someone who appreciates and tries to make what they value attractive to others.

§

None of this, of course, is easy. In addition to the pressures professors feel from a bad job market, from the voices of careerism, and from teaching in a time when the liberal arts are under attack, it can be hard to take heart knowing that one's commitment is played out on a very small stage and won and lost each day.[43] Though we are defending very big and very important ideas, texts, and ways of being together in an educative community, this defense happens in the here-and-now of our actual lived environment. That is, if my courses don't convince my current students that a liberal education is worth their time, it really makes no difference if I can plead my case before an ideal audience. Or, at least this is what Miller wants us to take seriously. In a complicated passage I won't be able to fully unpack in this chapter,[44] he writes:

> We are demoralized today because we proclaim liberty but no actuality as local control and as revelation. Nothing is to be revered. Here is no eloquent presence. . . . I want the actual to shine and I want to feel the wonder of a yardstick, a poem, a word, a person. The here-and-now appears to me quite dreamlike unless it can declare the world. I am glad that the dream is dispelled for me.[45]

This passage has the aphoristic-poetic style of much of Miller's best writing, and like his best writing it is deeply evocative. At the beginning of the last paragraph of his great essay "Experience," Emerson writes: "I know that the world I converse with in the city and in the farms, is not the world I *think*."[46] This line has to be in the back of Miller's mind when he wrote this passage. In "Experience," Emerson is trying to bridge the gap between his ideals and the world. Unable to bridge this gap, he feels ghostlike, living in the dreamlike state of ideals that cannot be realized in the world. He concludes the essay with the line, "the true romance which the world exists to realize, will be the transformation of genius into practical power."[47] I see Miller asserting to Emerson that he has realized this transformation of dream into practical power because he can see the actual *shine*. It is possible to assert a presence when one commits to exercising local control. When Miller presents the force of an idea or an author to students in a way that captivates them in here-and-now, he establishes an eloquent presence. It is no dream, the text shines. In trying to meet the students where they are, he allows them to shine in their presence as well.

As I've tried to stress in this chapter, existential knowledge and local control means taking responsibility for the world through our criticism and our care. When we seek the freedom of criticism unmoored from commitment, we lose out on tending to the things of this world. Professors can easily fall into the trap of wishing their students or their institutions were different without working to uncover the ways in which the actually existing already contains an eloquent presence they can draw morale from. Though the world of our institution is always imperfect, that doesn't mean we cannot establish a presence by cultivating the potential already in existence right before us.

Miller doesn't retreat into an ideal world or bring ideals down to the level of the ordinary. Instead, he idealizes the actual, because he can find things to revere at the level of the yardstick, or the poem, or the word, or the person. Here is how Miller makes the point in his Hobart address:

> All education must idealize the actual. That seems to me to be what is open to us to do in our time. We are not likely to feel that we can actualize the ideal. We are not sure what the ideal may be, nor, in any abstract formulation of it, is there likely to be agreement. But we may, I suggest, find in the process of growth some intimations of the form of our world and of the human spirit. For at the close of college studies one needs to capture that morale which gives authenticity to what has been done and assurance of its sequel.[48]

A key idea here is finding in the process of growth through the education we experienced in college an intimation of the form of our world and spirit. What I take this to mean is that when we come to realize how our mind and character were formed by education, we will appreciate the meaning of local control, and this will empower us to establish a presence in our own daily life. To authenticate the process of making sense of a difficult text or idea is to prove to ourselves that we are capable of continued growth. We take something that feels like a conflict—a poem that just doesn't make sense, a person who seems foreign to us because we disagree so deeply with them—and somehow bring them into our orbit. Instead of standing ghostlike in front of an idea or a person, we establish a presence. I understand you, and I want to make sense of what our disagreement means, here and now. The poem speaks to me in this moment, and I now feel empowered to meet difficult texts and ideas, trusting that I am capable of coming to understanding because I met the challenge of understanding in the past.

Miller, as professor, stands as the sequel to the liberal education his students are receiving. A piece of trivia one learns while studying Miller is that he didn't own a car and lived within a very short walk of where he taught, rarely taking trips to even the closest town.[49] He is a placed man, and he finds power, he establishes a presence, by accepting his place and living his commitments from here. A term that didn't fully make sense to me until studying Miller was *rooted cosmopolitanism*.[50] Miller is completely devoted to the life of Williams College and his students, but this doesn't make him parochial or narrow-minded. When he reads the local newspaper or when he engages with faculty affairs on campus, he sees in these local things all the concerns that also animate the largest philosophical discourses. Unlike the scholar who only feels fulfilled speaking at the level of scholarship, discovering what Plato's text means for anyone who reads him, Miller seeks to understand the meaning of Plato in the life of a small village in the Berkshires and in the life of an eighteen-year-old who is experiencing higher education for the first time.

The risk of doing this is that one never becomes a scholar of note. Miller published very little during his life, and even from the excerpts of his work shared in this chapter, one can tell that his idiom is unique. In a very strange piece of coincidence, my undergraduate advisor Stanley Bates reviewed one of Miller's posthumously published books and made the case that there is something very compelling about Miller, but that he is impossible to place within the landscape of current philosophical concern.[51] I think this was due, in large part, to the fact that to understand Miller you must understand that he placed himself squarely in the local: in his life as a teacher at Williams College. But far from discounting him from saying something of broader significance, being placed gives Miller a powerful voice that deserves our hearing.

Miller speaks with an authentic presence to those of us who also find ourselves willing to accept that we don't teach anywhere; we teach at our own institutions with their own histories and with our own students who have their own interests and strengths.[52] Instead of crafting a writerly persona that can speak broadly in the voice of scholarship that can be easily assimilated by other scholars wherever they are placed, Miller establishes a presence that we must contend with. This might partially explain why his work is still looking for an audience, but it also explains why it made him just what his students needed. He was present with them; an educative presence who empowered them to ground themselves in their work at college.

I will expand this point in the final chapter, but I feel our students need this type of presence now more than ever. The lure of social media and other forms of technology are powerful.[53] If a lecture begins to get boring or slow to students, they can absent themselves into the world of their phone or their desire to be on their phone. More, many of our students may have been raised in homes where their parents were similarly engaged with their phones and not present. I often cannot think of a better defense of liberal education than that it promises students presence. We have small classes and very hands-on advising, because although a student can certainly read about all of the graduation requirements online, there is something reassuring about being present with an advisor, talking through the point of these requirements, and the ways they can become meaningful for the student.[54] Just as the students at Williams loved seeing Miller walking to campus, our students like to see us walking campus without our heads down in our phones. They like someone who is a presence on campus and present in the classroom. I will not downplay the pressures we are under as professors, but I will also assert that our students need us to be present, and we need to find ways to establish ourselves as educative presences on our campuses.

If Miller is right, we do this by critically living our commitments in the here-and-now. We seek to live the concerns that animate the writers and thinkers we care most about in the here-and-now, taking the faculty meeting or the advising session as places where we establish presence, treating them with the moral seriousness they deserve. Though these can seem like distractions from our real work as scholars, Miller shows us that the advising session or the committee meeting on graduation requirements are places where we establish ourselves as scholars-in-the-world. By exercising local control, we establish a presence.

§

In the next chapter I introduce notes on the liberal arts Miller wrote in response to conversations occurring at Williams. Though these notes were written out of local concern, they are examples of something that can also speak authentically to the broader significance of liberal education and its continuing importance. Miller's placed presence gives him a unique authority to speak to the meaning of liberal education, and I find it a valuable contribution to the already large literature on the topic.

Though these notes were written in 1943 and Miller's Hobart address was delivered nine years later, the line of thinking I develop around presence and morale in this chapter equally applies to the 1943 piece offered in the next chapter. Miller is a teacher with presence and a teacher of presence. I find this his biggest contribution to how we can think about liberal education in our time. A teacher with presence has morale and inspires morale in students. Miller's notes on liberal education help us think about how we can establish an educative presence for students, and I will return to this theme in my commentary on these notes and in my final chapter when I draw out what Miller's thinking might mean to those of us who teach at liberal arts colleges or who see ourselves as trustees of the value of this form of educating.

CHAPTER TWO

REFLECTIONS ON THE LIBERAL EDUCATION

Note: It is unclear to me if these notes were ever delivered in a public form. They are dated 1943. In the folder where the notes can be found, a program for a conference on the liberal arts hosted by Williams College was also included, but John William Miller is not on the program. My feeling is that this essay was Miller's contribution to conversations around that conference and served as a foundation for his thinking on the liberal arts that he would draw on in his teaching and committee work at Williams. The essay is found in box 2, folder 9, in the Miller Collection housed at the Williams College library. Section 1 to the conclusion were typed. After the typed essay, Miller handwrote section 11. I transcribed section 11. There are a few words that were unclear to me as I did this transcription, so I had to use my judgment when putting it together. As well, Miller gives this handwritten section the number 11, but its theme is closer to that of section 6. I discuss section 6 and 11 together in my commentary.

REFLECTIONS ON THE LIBERAL EDUCATION

(1) The liberal education is not defined through subject matter.

Any branch of knowledge can be learned in a liberal or in a non-liberal way. For example, history may become the vehicle of dogma or indoctrination. Science and mathematics, central elements in the liberal education, may be presented as vocationally useful information. When this happens, history and science lose their liberal quality.

§

(2) The liberal education is not defined as knowledge of fact or of operations.

All operations require skills, sometimes more than is supposed. It takes training to make a square cut with a saw, to spell, to cook, to swim, to speak a foreign tongue. All knowledge is power; but not all power breeds liberality of mind. The training of animals enlarges their powers, but it also leaves them slaves of their masters and of the signals which prompt their activities.

§

(3) The liberal education is defined in the various forms of self-control, when these are identified as such.

Knowledge brings mastery; but it may be only a mastery of materials. That is not liberal. Liberal education must at every point show the bearing of various types of knowledge on the integrity of mind and will. And this integrity must be seen as one's own demand, as the meaning of personality.

§

(4) Integrity is not itself an instrumental value, but is the condition for the vigorous and determined prosecution of special purposes.

Integrity is an immediate and intrinsic value. The search for it may even get one into trouble. It often has. The liberal education can make men; it cannot promise to make them rich, powerful, honored or happy. Many persons resist the demands of the liberal education because they cannot surrender to the disinterested. They prefer to be "practical." It should require no argument to say that efficiency and benevolence are themselves corollaries of the liberal spirit, not its essence.

§

(5) The appeal of the liberal education is exerted by the promise of power. This promise resides in a lawful, and hence dynamic, subject matter and in the minds which possessed the vigor and the tensions capable of producing it. It promises association with those creative minds.

Liberality lives chiefly in its exemplars. Religions, for instance, illustrate the power of persons. Many who do not understand the technical theology which concerned the Council of Nicea nevertheless "believe" in the creed. The liberal man, like the religious man, can believe only where there is mystery. Foolish men confound mystery with obscurantism, whereas mystery is rather promise, and the unfolding of promise into new revelation and new powers. Unfortunately good men, and great men, have been degraded because they have been presented as more logical, more shrewd, or more informed rather than as free and self-contained spirits whose adventurous temper we need to make our own. Great intellect is only great passion in good form. This is just as true for mathematics as for philosophy or literature.

§

(6) Saving institutions called liberal arts colleges is not the same as saving liberal education. A good many illiberal liberal arts colleges can look forward to a tolerably assured future.

§

(7) A proper conception of the liberal education is of first importance to teachers, and to their morale.

The teachers of the liberal arts know that they have nothing to offer except the intrinsic worth of critical adventure. Let them be given the impression that a college exists for any purpose of a special sort and they face conflict within themselves. There is no particular good to be derived from Plato, or Shakespeare, or Emerson, or Einstein. These are disinterested minds and their meaning is lost in so far as one is not prepared to walk in their steps, however remotely.

§

(8) There is no point of view not defined by the liberal attitude which can recommend the liberal education.

It would seem that no statement about the meaning of the liberal education, including this one, can be hopefully undertaken. The presentation of such statements will bring either a deep agreement beyond argument, or else an equally deep disagreement likewise beyond argument. But this outcome has a great use, namely to make plain what was above suggested; that at the last one confronts men and not ideas, and that the authority of various views develops freely from the pattern of a personal integrity and power. Consequently, one must go one's way. This is the residual risk of the liberal. But the hope of eventual agreement lies precisely in the sort of fateful experiences which the disinterested mind invites. The practice of freedom can alone disclose its form and its laws.

§

(9) There is no affirmative way of dealing with the technical and practical problems of curricula and of instructional devises. One can only remove the hindrances to the attainment of liberal outlooks.

Administrators sometimes exhibit undue optimism. Yet the constant changing of educational techniques should be enough to end the hope of a curricular utopia. One can say no more than this, that some arrangements impede study or dispel its atmosphere. As in law, one must proceed here by discovering hindrances to freedom, rather than fixing its form in some affirmative way.

One need not reject the value of technical innovation in the construction of curricula. Yet, on the whole, the history of education lies in the expansion and organization of subject matter then in mechanical changes. For example, the plan of study at the University of Michigan in 1843 to 1844 (Cubberley, "Readings in the History of Education," 590–91), is now quite outmoded.[55] It is outmoded by the advance of organized knowledge. Any curricular scheme will leave it imperative to study those concepts, figures and works which define some lawful subject matter. Nothing can change that.

No one engaged in liberal teaching should expect all practical arrangements to suit his taste. But practical arrangements will inevitably reflect the view of personal living which administrators entertain and embody. When the offering of courses, the balance of departments or the scheduling of classes is the care of men whose own outlook and personal habits are reflective, modest and humane, one can trust the result. Education is a social or historical symbol as much as art or science. It is this only because one can read off character from arrangements. They are corollaries of character, never the work of detached reason. If education produces character, it should never be forgotten that it also proceeds from character.

§

(10) I propose that colleges take themselves seriously as the vehicle of community.

For a free country, the concept of community does not consist in agreement on specific truths, but rather on the form of these. Colleges may serve society, but that is a by-product. Their authority will be obscure if they see this authority beyond themselves. It must reside in them. They must exemplify in their studies and ceremonies the secular authority of thought.

This is a large theme. It may be obscured by expansion in this place. But I notice the growing importance of the problem of morale, in the nation and in the schools. And it may be ventured that morale can occur only apropos of something intrinsic, a present value, sportive and severe. If the liberal education is not now the vehicle of morale, what is?

§

Summary:
Since a person's ideas on education reflect his general sense of values, argument for any one program is not likely to be effective. Something has to be left to destiny. In any case, the liberal spirit, if it is to survive and grow must be attractive. This attraction lies in its promise of power. But this power must consist in personal freedom and self-knowledge, and this, in turn, must take the form of a quest for laws. Laws and their exemplars alone possess steady prestige, for they are the loci of both control and growth.

§

(II) The liberal teacher must take care to present only as much as the student can appropriate in his will and understanding.

There is some disproportion between the amount of time spent on history, literature, philosophy etc. and the student's feeling of proprietorship over such materials. Teachers want to "cover the ground" and they can give the appearance of having done so because most students possess considerable competence in acquiring information, words and phrases. The average undergraduate creates the illusion of liberal advance because his intelligence permits facility in memory work. Yet he may have understood very little. Especially is this appearance of liberalism likely to result when the materials studied seems by itself to guarantee an emancipated mind. Yet there is no more liberalism in the *Communist Manifesto* than in the prophecy of Jeremiah; no more in Lenin than in Gregory the Great. Nothing is liberal in effect unless it can become a calm possession of a confident mind. No one has a liberal education because he has studied "liberal" rather than "illiberal" doctrines or movements. Because many do not make this distinction our liberals are so often unapproachable in their dogmatism. The liberal education does not teach men to be in any partisan sense "liberals." The partisan liberal or radical too often shows that he has only learned his lessons, not that he has understood his beliefs or professions. In sum, it is dangerous to carry the humanities beyond the point where their content loses meaning in the actually established values of the student. The "humane" and "liberal" education has too often upset character and muddled polities.

CHAPTER THREE

EXTENDED COMMENTARY

Each of these short sub-chapters explores a section or sections of Miller's notes on liberal education.

SECTIONS 1-3: GROUNDWORK

The first three sections of "Reflections on the Liberal Education" establish a groundwork that Miller will build from. It is tempting to read these sections quickly, especially as they don't appear to break any significant ground. Section 1 reminds the reader that there is a difference between liberal education and vocational training. Section 2 expands the point, going so far as to draw a parallel between the training of animals and skills-based teaching and learning. In section 3, Miller connects liberal education to self-cultivation. Again, it doesn't seem as if Miller is breaking new ground, but a closer read may prove otherwise.

What is striking about section 1 is the very first sentence: "The liberal education is not defined through subject matter." It is important to appreciate that this would be controversial to many of the staunchest defenders of the liberal arts.[56] To some, the liberal arts *is* the curriculum, if not a very specific set of great books. For this reason, certain subjects—teacher education, law, business—are automatically not appropriate subjects for liberal study, while other subjects—classics, philosophy, literature—automatically are.[57] I was a new assistant professor at Sweet Briar College when we were having discussions about how to save the college in the face of grave financial difficulties that ultimately led to a decision to close the school. Though this decision was overturned, what stood out most to me as a new professor was the sense in the Sweet Briar community that we wanted to be saved as a liberal arts college. But, as we had discussions about what this meant, it become apparent that some members of the faculty saw the liberal arts as courses and majors that students must take, while others saw them as more in line with Miller's thinking in section 1. Someone could study English illiberally, just as someone could became a liberally educated teacher.[58] Though liberal education may be more naturally at home in certain fields of study than others, it would be a mistake to automatically credit or discount entire fields of study as liberal or illiberal.[59]

As well, it is important to appreciate how Miller is an example of someone who is a staunch defender of liberal education, but not necessarily an advocate of great books. All too often the great books, or canon, debate becomes a flashpoint, with advocates of the great books lamenting their neglect and critics of great books claiming that they enshrine dead white males as the only thing worth studying. Instead of taking sides in this debate, we might turn our attention back to Emerson. In "The American Scholar," and as discussed in the previous chapter, Emerson makes the point: "Books are the best of things, well used; abused, among the worst."[60] This strikes me as a key point that defenders and detractors of the liberal arts tend to ignore. Though it is very useful to draw a line of connection from small liberal arts colleges in America to their forerunners in Europe, the American liberal arts college is also very much its own thing.[61] Though our curriculum and our ideals are borrowed from Europe, they are also very much, and uniquely, in the American grain. Emerson follows his thinking on books with the lines: "What is the right use? What is the one end, which all means go to effect? They are for nothing but to inspire."[62] Though liberal education can trace its roots back to older ideals, Emerson's insight about the connection between education and inspiration is another way of thinking about the liberal arts college in America. We were inventing a system of schools and ways of thinking fit for our unique American ideals, history, and contradictions, and we needed inspired men and women to take up this work. I worry that this sounds too much like American exceptionalism, but I feel it is worth stressing that as much as the great books or a set curriculum feels necessary in order to call a college liberal, I think this also fails to appreciate the unique history and nature of American liberal arts colleges.

Books are to inspire new thinking; they aren't items that one must master in order to call oneself liberally educated. Though this line of thinking brings with it the risk of philistinism or antiintellectualism—and Americans have been called this and much worse—this needn't be the case. Emerson begins by stating that books are the best of things, and he means it. A liberal education will involve a great deal of reading, but much of this reading will be in the service of inspiring a student to take responsibility for their own interests and concerns. An education should put a student in conversation with the greatest books that speak to those interests and concerns, but if they fail to read some authors or great books in the process, I don't see the need to take away the title of "liberally educated" from them. Books are used to inspire, not to demarcate the liberally educated from the masses.

I worry that as a liberal education comes under increased scrutiny for its "return on investment" we will fall into two unhelpfully divided camps. The one camp will do anything to attract students, adding new majors without considering how they can be taught in liberal ways, with the other group refusing to consider the possibility that a subject like business can be taught liberally.[63] I hope we can avoid this unhelpful dualistic thinking, just as I hope we can appreciate Emerson's thinking on books. Instead of treating a book as if it was inherently good or bad, we should give students the experience of feeling the presence of what the book inspires, only then determining its worth. We should aim to show the continued value of great books through the ways they inspire new thoughts, while remaining vigilant in the quest to make sure we are bringing the best books to students, a process that will inevitably and productively make the canon more inclusive.

Avoiding internal debates that become unhelpful is a value, because liberal arts colleges are increasingly contending with the rise of credentialism, and the pressures of credentialism will have to be met or they could seriously undermine liberal education. A student came into my office a few days before graduation last year lamenting the rise of regalia cords. At one point, a time not so long ago, students who made Phi Beta Kappa were allowed to wear something at graduation marking them as members of the honor society. Very recently, students began adding new cords: cords for study abroad, cords for clubs, cords for majors. I don't bring this up to be a crank, but rather because it is illustrative of a bigger issue. Students are being taught to see their education as something of an arms race where more is almost always seen as better. For example, when I meet with first-year students for advising, many plan to double major and double minor and study abroad multiple times. I see this drive coming from two related places: a desire to get the most from an expensive education, and a desire to be competitive in the job market. The problem with this way of thinking is that a liberal arts education is not like Supermarket Sweep. One subject, a handful of books, and a big idea studied well can be much better preparation for a job or a life than an accumulation approach to education. Just as a liberal education isn't defined through subject matter, it isn't defined through numbers of majors and minors.

The pressure to acquire or to flatten an education to a credential is very real, and I appreciate why parents and students would worry about getting the most from their liberal education. We need to do more to help these worried parents and students appreciate some of the higher ideals behind the liberal education they are investing money in so that they might receive its broadest benefits. I think Miller helps us do this. And I can only encourage those of us who care about liberal education, as busy as we are, to do everything we can to talk with parents and students about the limitations of credentialism and the ways in which a liberal education, as experienced in the here-and-now by students, can empower them to pursue meaningful work after graduation in whatever field they enter.

One way to think about meaningful work is to revisit section 2 of "Reflections on the Liberal Education." The key line, and it is a powerful one, is: "All knowledge is power; but not all power breeds liberality of mind." As he notes immediately following this line, a well-trained animal experiences new powers, but these powers make the animal dependent on the master or the stimulus the master provides. Here, I don't think Miller is equating vocational education with animal training. Instead, I see him asking us to think about the foundational aims of an education. Though it may feel empowering to experience mastery of information that can be immediately put to use, the way in which one acquires this power also needs to be considered. This can be a very hard lesson to learn and to teach. For example, many students want the types of skills that employers want. One of these skills is the use of Microsoft Excel. The thing I struggle with, as an educator, is thinking about how the skillful use of Excel can be taught. Can it be taught in a liberal way or is it a skill that one is trained to acquire: a power that one gains. Because a student knows exactly what they want—this very specific skill with Excel—I have a hard time seeing how it can be taught in a liberal way. By contrast, the skill of leading a classroom discussion—a skill all future teachers will need—is something that can be taught liberally.[64] It can be taught liberally, because the *person* enacting the skill has a great influence on how the skill is enacted, and because there is more than one way to enact this skill virtuously, the teacher must always exercise judgment to run a discussion well.[65] Learning the skill of artful classroom discussion involves the future teacher learning about who they are and what they value as an educator. I can't see the same opportunities for liberal education when a student learns Excel. This is not to say that our students shouldn't learn Excel or that it isn't essential for certain jobs. My question is what role this type of skills training should play as part of a liberal education. For example, could we help students find ways of teaching this skill to themselves while also helping them appreciate why a college classroom may not be the best place to learn it? Would this allow them to gain a valuable skill while deepening their appreciation for liberal education?

The pressure of credentialism also makes it feel like we never have enough time to do everything, so if a student can learn a necessary skill—Excel—and get academic credit for it, that is an ideal outcome for the credentialist. As such, it is difficult to convince a student that they should do something—learn Excel—on their own time, and devote their academic credits to liberal education. Similar to the profession of teaching, judgment seems unavoidable in most fields of business, from accounting to management. It seems important to show students that though the feeling of immediate power one gains through learning Excel feels satisfying, it pales in comparison to learning how to become the type of person who knows what types of ends are worth using Excel to accomplish: that is, a person who knows what to value and how. It pales in comparison, in large part, because a person who selects between competing ends has to think through who they are and what is worth their commitment. A liberal education helps a student do this, and no online tutorial can. Business in the liberal education curriculum can cultivate judgment, though it should be wary of directly teaching narrow skills that a student can learn quite easily on their own.[66]

Part of becoming liberally educated means knowing the

difference between skills we can acquire and questions we must live. Part of what it means to be a trustee of this form of education is making sure that students learn this difference. We don't do this by denigrating their desire to learn Excel or by providing them with in-class experiences that can be replicated by an online tutorial.[67] What is needed is giving students the experience of presence, of being in the presence of a truly complicated and engaging idea, of being present with other students and a professor who are trying to make meaning of that idea. When a student learns how to learn what they feel about a complicated or controversial issue, and I hope this isn't being overly optimistic, they can also learn that they are capable of teaching themselves Excel or any other skill in an on-demand way. The point is giving them the experience of struggling to discover what they believe or what their beliefs mean (knowing there are often multiple good answers to any complex question) and living with the consequences. When a student has this experience, they will turn to the books and discussions that actually help them think, and they will begin realizing the qualitative difference between liberal education and mere skill acquisition. More, a student will appreciate that they should demand so much more from their liberal education than learning skills that they can teach themselves.

This brings us to Miller's third point, where he connects liberal education to self-control. A liberally educated person exercises various forms of self-control, and this sense of self-control connects to a person's integrity, which Miller will discuss further in section 4. What strikes me as important, from section 3, is the idea that mastery of materials does not make someone liberally educated. Here, again, I find myself returning to Emerson in order to understand Miller. The difference between self-reliance and mere conformity is central to Emerson's thinking. The conformist does what it takes to succeed given the rules of the game as they are established by society. They master the tools and materials needed for success, but they never consider what this means for their self-worth and never connect this to a larger philosophy of life. By contrast, the person who exercises self-reliance may appear odd by, or at odds with, conformists, but this is because they exercise thought. Though they are clever enough to master the game of school, or the game of society, they see through these games and want to know their purpose and how they will form their personality. They do this not to please anyone else; it is a demand coming from them: a demand to be themselves and no one else.

Miller's and Emerson's thinking bring out one of the biggest tensions in liberal education, which is how education for self-reliance is even possible.[68] We are unavoidably influenced by the powerful presences we experience in books and in our teachers. As such, it can be hard to know if we are influenced by an idea or an opinion out of conformity or because we actually assent to the idea. This is one of my biggest fears when teaching undergraduates. I worry that the positive experience a student has in one of my classes may make them unduly interested in what I am interested in, without considering how they really feel about the topic. There have been times when students were registering for my classes without reading the course title or description: they just wanted to take another class with me. I think the experience is common for professors, but it is troubling nonetheless. One of the things that is comforting about equating liberal education with a curriculum or a set of books or a skill is that we can teach these things with a clear conscience. But if liberal education is really about freeing students for self-education so that their education can "at every point show the bearing of various types of knowledge on the integrity of mind and will" we must always be on guard, lest we unintentional coerce a student down a pathway that leads them away from their own interests and into conformity with ours.

I began my commentary on these sections suggesting that there were more to them than may initially appear and I hope I've made good on that suggestion. If liberal education is about empowering a student for something like self-reliance, or what Miller calls integrity, it makes our work as professors that much harder. What we cannot do is teach skills, because these skills don't allow students to form purposes. Someone who merely enacts a skill without a sense of purpose is a conformist and not liberally educated. But if purposes must be discovered through education, we must be aware, as professors, of the difference between freeing a student to discover the meaning of their own education and unintentionally doing that work for them. As often as possible, we must give students the room to practice self-criticism and self-reflection, having them ask: What does this new skill, or new understanding mean for my sense of what is valuable? Who would I become if I believed *x*, or found *y* beautiful or good? What options do I foreclose by devoting myself to this cause, or this idea, or this way of thinking? By providing space for students to live these questions—alone, in community with other students, and through our feedback and instruction—we give them the experience of liberal education.

SECTION 4: INTEGRITY

Section 4 offers a compressed but impassioned statement of the value of becoming liberally educated. It is worth taking some time with the opening sentence: "Integrity is not itself an instrumental value, but is the condition for the vigorous and determined prosecution of special purposes." To start, it is hard not to hear echoes of Immanuel Kant in Miller's use of instrumental value.[69] In the previous chapter, I discuss Emerson's thinking on self-reliance and conformity; standing behind Emerson is the towering influence of Kant.[70] Kant famously drew a distinction between autonomy and heteronomy, which can—very roughly—track Emerson's distinction between self-reliance and conformity. The goal for Kant and Emerson—and also Miller—is to empower a student to think for themselves. The student should act only on reasons they can assent to after giving them due consideration; they shouldn't act on reasons just because they are socially acceptable or convenient.

Emerson and Kant also warn that to exercise autonomy or self-reliance is to risk putting oneself at odds with society, because society values conformity and punishes independent thinkers. Kant worried that heteronomous, or conformist, thinking often leads us to devalue what we should treasure, causing us to pursue ends that aren't worthy of our humanity. Here, Kant draws his famous distinction between value and price. Humanity has value, while things have a price.[71] We often forget this, as when we use crude versions of cost-benefit analyses that give human lives a price (and, often, a very negligible one at that) to make decisions. To take a recent and very egregious example, when civic leaders in Michigan neglected their duty to protect the people of Flint by allowing them to drink toxic water, they devalued the humanity of the people of Flint. The people of Flint were used as a means to save money; they were not taken seriously as ends in themselves or as the source of unlimited value.

Miller tells us that integrity is not an instrumental value, declaring it—following Kant and Emerson—something beyond price. Our integrity is a source of value, and we must come to appreciate this fact. Education, then, must always be responsive to our integrity, otherwise it cheapens into something that has a mere price. (Here I don't miss the irony that liberal education does have a price and a very expensive one, but the thing Kant helps us see is that something with a price always makes it interchangeable with other things with a price, and this is not quite the case when it comes to the value of education. At places committed to liberal education, we aren't just marching students through commercially produced PowerPoint slides, giving them an experience that they can have anywhere. We are using our presence—something that only exists here, with this group of students and in this place—to educate.) More, our integrity is the condition for *vigorous* and *determined* action. Or, to use the language of the introduction, integrity is fundamental for the development of morale. When we take up the work of discovering what we value, what we are willing to critically commit ourselves to, we experience what it means to have integrity. Doing the work of establishing integrity also then empowers us with morale so that we can move through the world with determination and vigor.

Miller goes on: "Integrity is an immediate and intrinsic value. The search for it may even get one into trouble. It often has. The liberal education can make men; it cannot promise to make them rich, powerful, honored or happy." Here Miller is very clearly echoing Kant on autonomy and Emerson on self-reliance, repeating the idea that integrity has value, but when we value it, we are not promised success in the world where things have a price. We can think of very extreme cases where this is true: civil rights activists who risk everything because they see the value of humanity. Their refusal to be dehumanized or contribute to dehumanizing policies and practices make them a target of scorn, hatred, violence, and death. On a much smaller scale, and one familiar to teachers, I think we are a profession committed to integrity, often to the detriment of material success. Many of the teachers and professors I know could be very successful in fields that would earn them significantly more money, and yet they commit tremendous care and time to making a child or a young person feel welcome in the classroom. Eschewing efficiency thinking or any sense of cost-benefit analysis, they take the time to be present with children and young people in a way that very clearly communicates the child's worth and intrinsic value. This causes the teacher to "lose" by the lights of price-based accounting, but their integrity creates and sustains value in the world.

Here, too, is a place where we can develop and draw on morale. A teacher has the power to free a student to take themselves seriously in a way that they did not know was possible. A teacher, by giving a young person the space and support to think, can empower them to turn away from conformity and to a recognition of their integrity and intrinsic worth. And, a teacher can gain morale from this. As they free students to do vigorous and determined work, they are reminded of why liberal education matters.

§

The liberally educated person doesn't just run the risk of losing in terms of material success, they risk appearing ineffectual. Someone who teaches a group of students to appreciate and understand something that Toni Morrison writes is not making an immediate political or practical difference in the world. Someone who helps a student understand a complicated philosophical argument or religious ritual also doesn't make a direct political or practical impact. We know that higher education is often disparaged as an ivory tower, or—as I hear my students describe it—a bubble. Though many really nice things happen in the bubble, what happens in the bubble doesn't actually impact the so-called real world. Though it is tempting to respond to this type of critique by connecting the dots from a close reading of *Beloved* to a well-developed moral or political sensibility, I am not sure how convincing this would be or how honest. I think we all know that there are many benefits to reading an author like Morrison, but I also think we know the difference between work that has an immediate political impact (canvassing, registering voters, attending local board meetings) and the work we do in the classroom, where the overriding goals are understanding and appreciation, not an action leading to a clear and often predetermined end.

This background is useful to have in mind when considering Miller's thoughts on the practical. He writes, "Many persons resist the demands of the liberal education because they cannot surrender to the disinterested. They prefer to be 'practical.'" Miller already touched on the difference between vocational training and liberal education, but here he is drawing our attention to the distinction between the disinterested and the practical. I find this distinction useful to keep in mind, especially in light of recent attempts to make liberal education more relevant. Here I am not thinking of offering courses that are marketable for a career, but courses that are meant to dissolve the lines between the academy and the world. These types of courses empower students to use what they are learning in class to respond to real problems. For example, in a course students may learn about water pollution, how to measure for water pollution, how to respond when water is polluted, and then test local lakes and rivers. In this way, the students can see their educations in action. We can think of many other examples: students learning about voter suppression and then helping register voters; learning about digital ethnographies and then completing these for a local historical organization; students learning about lack of affordable childcare in the community and learning how to write policy and opinion pieces, or volunteering at a local Head Start center to address the issue.

These types of courses are important and have a place at liberal arts colleges. What Miller's thinking reminds us of is the need to connect these practical experiences and the student's own growing sense of integrity. That is, the student volunteering at the Head Start center may see the connection between that experience and the course itself, but it is unclear what type of critical self-reflection the student can engage in because of the experience. If there is really one response—such as, this situation is bad and I need to do something about it—we may wonder what the practical component of the course added to the student's liberal education. This may be an unfair reading of these types of courses. I bring it up so that we might consider the impact of including practical experiences as parts of courses at liberal arts college, and wonder if they are, intentionally or not, a hindrance to the type of disinterested study Miller identifies as central to liberal education. That is, I am concerned that the desire to make liberal education practical might undercut the very values that liberal education is uniquely positioned to teach students.

I worry that disinterested study can come to be seen as a vice, either by detractors of the academy or by those within who want students to experience the power of what they are learning in the world as a means to supporting the contemporary significance of liberal education. Disinterested study needn't be equated with apathy, when its goal is giving students access to a different realm of value than those already accredited with importance. We know it is important to get a job, just as we know it is important to make a difference in the world. I would not say the same of figuring out who we are and what we believe after study and reflection. To return to my criticism of philosophical thought experiments developed in the introduction, *disinterested*, in the way Miller uses it, means giving yourself the time to consider an idea, a text, or a conversation, and let it educate you, even if you aren't fully in control of where this type of thinking might lead you. This is a dangerous state to be in, because a liberal who seriously considers Edmund Burke or Michael Oakeshott may discover they resonate with conservatism. They may or may not stay that way, but the experience of realizing the power of thought to unsettle their identity touches on the connection between liberal education and integrity in a profound way. The experience of disinterested study teaches us that we are capable of deep change, change that is often unpredictable and unsettling.

A liberally educated person doesn't hold beliefs dogmatically, and I see disinterestedness, in Miller's sense, as something of a practice or a way of living. With the rise of social media, students are overwhelmed by having to take sides on any and every issue. They have to take an interest in everything, and this is leaving them with no time to reflect on bigger questions. As such, disinterestedness, in the hyperconnected world students live in, strikes me as less like apathy and more like an act of resistance.[72] Instead of forcing a student to take a side, we give them space to let an issue or text educate. We give the student time to consider what something means before we offer them practical experience with the issue. Instead of seeing the bubble of the college campus as a liability, we use it to our advantage by freeing students to learn the habit of disinterested study. To be disinterested is to be practiced in the art of ongoing self-criticism, ever vigilant lest we slip into mere conformity, where we give opinions on things we don't truly care about or know enough to develop a considered position on. Integrity is established by allowing ourselves the space for disinterested study, a space where we try to establish freedom from conformity and freedom for commitment to what we value.

§

In the final sentence of section 4 Miller establishes corollaries of disinterestedness. Though the aim of liberal study is not the acquisition of practical skills, "efficiency and benevolence are themselves corollaries of the liberal spirit." I find this fascinating. Reading the full sentence, the tone seems negative, because he asserts that efficiency and benevolence are *not* the essence of liberal study. But he chooses corollary very intentionally to show that we cannot help but become more efficient and benevolent through liberal education.

I won't dwell on this point at length, but here Miller reminds us of the importance of trusting liberal education. Though it doesn't aim for efficiency or benevolence, if a student gives themselves over to disinterested study, these will also be achieved. How is this? To start, someone habituated to disinterested thought doesn't see change, or the new, as an immediate threat. It becomes an opportunity to exercise thought. A person who is willing to consider all sides of an issue gets used to seeing the limitations of their current view of the world. This type of person, when confronted with a problem, is better able to adapt because they have developed the habit of disinterested thought. Though the work of considering different interpretations of a text may seem utterly impractical, Miller is right to remind us that this habit will make us more efficient in the world, because we have learned how to be adaptable. Disinterested study breaks the fight/flight mindset, preparing us to adapt to new, often unforeseeable challenges.

In the same way liberal study makes a student efficient when facing a changing and ever-challenging world, it can also make them benevolent. Here, I think of another line from the closing paragraph of Emerson's "Experience." He writes: "It takes a good deal of time to eat or to sleep, or to earn a hundred dollars, and a very little time to entertain a hope and an insight which becomes the light of our life."[73] A student giving themselves over to disinterested study goes into the process of reading a book or listening to an argument open to learning. Though we know it takes a great deal of time and effort to make a large sum of money, if we open ourselves up to learning from experience, we may discover—in an instant—the light of our life. I hope students at liberal arts colleges have this experience in abundance. Every class meeting should be an opening to wonder; each book, each assignment should be a chance to be surprised at just how interesting the world is. This experience of wonder often provokes gratitude and a sense of benevolence. When we realize the riches that lie in wait in what is freely available in any public library—and available in complete abundance on our college campus—we begin to see that we can give our own gifts more freely. We can be less stingy with our resources, realizing that there are sources of goodness and unlimited value available to anyone who claims the power of disinterested study. This is all very Emersonian, and it may be too much for the taste of some readers. In response, I can only assert that we shouldn't lose sight of the profound and life-changing joy that comes when we are moved by a text, a piece of music, a conversation. Here, I am thinking especially of those moments that happen outside of class, in the unique type of leisure that occurs on college campuses.[74] When students have the time to talk and appreciate the natural and built beauty of the world around them, they begin to break out of a mindset that assigns a price to everything, and are open to the world of value that is waiting from them. When they continue a conversation, when they pick up a new interest, when they linger while looking at a painting or contemplating the aims of the education they are receiving, they enter a new realm of meaning.

Liberal education can remind students that they are beyond price. It reminds students that they have value and can achieve integrity. In a world intent on commodifying everything, it is good that there are still spaces where this aspect of our humanity is recognized and cultivated. Though cynicism and fear are in no short supply, someone who believes in the innate integrity of other people, of students particularly, should not be scoffed at or written off as out of touch with the hard realities of our world.[75] In fact, these types of people have morale and establish a presence that we should recognize as central to the vocation of liberal education.[76] These teachers persist in maintaining a world of value that is threatened. They tend the fields of study so that students can develop responsibility for directing their own education.

SECTION 5: MYSTERY AND ADVENTURE

When liberal education is flattened to mere credentialism, we lose the spirit of adventure that is at its heart. Section 5 seeks to remedy this by asserting the ways in which a liberal education is provoked by mystery, which leads to an adventure that results in increased power on the part of the adventurer. As the previous sections make clear, the power one gains through liberal education is not achieved when one aims for narrowly vocational or practical ends. Rather, liberal education works by intimation and aspiration. When a student glimpses the promises held in store by this education, through their reading or conversations, they can give themselves over to this form of education, trusting that it will be empowering. With other forms of education, trust is not required. If someone promises to teach me how to use Microsoft Excel, I either learn to use it or demand a refund.

Liberal education is different, in large part, because the person undergoing the education will influence the direction the education takes. It is unhelpful to compare a student receiving a liberal education to a consumer, because a liberal education is not a simple transaction.[77] Getting into a college and paying tuition is only the first step. The more a student invests in their education the greater their "returns" will be. Where a product we purchase almost always begins depreciating the moment we buy it—technology becomes antiquated, a new model car is already in production—an education is something that becomes more expansive and valuable the more we commit ourselves to it.[78] Though the promise offered by a guarantee will often seem like a better bargain, it is important for students to understand that a guarantee will only give them what they are capable of imagining at an earlier stage of their development. A liberal education, by contrast, becomes more rewarding; it is capable of growing with you as you become more educated. If you come into college without much confidence in your potential, you will often aim too low. A liberal education will teach a student to aim much higher, and it thus allows them to enter professions that they would've never imagined as options before they experienced this form of education.[79]

This is why Miller reminds us, at the start of section 5, that the appeal of liberal education is in its promise of power. It offers a promise, but not a guarantee. We trust the promise of liberal education because it seems to offer us the possibility of greater power than if we set our sights lower, assuming that we know, as a high school student, the trajectory our life will take, and that college will just offer us a track to that life. Instead of choosing to narrow ourselves to a track chosen in high school, we take a leap of faith. We choose a form of education that will mandate we take courses outside of our areas of interest and chosen fields of study, trusting that this will somehow be for the best.

Here, the platitude that a liberal education makes a student well-rounded needs to be placed next to the faith students show by choosing a liberal education. It is not enough to tell a student that taking a series of courses unrelated to their areas of interest will make them well-rounded, as if this was a justification worthy of their faith. We need something more, and this is what Miller offers in the second sentence of section 5. He writes: "This promise [the promise of power] resides in a lawful, and hence dynamic, subject matter and in the minds which possessed the vigor and the tensions capable of producing it." To clear up any initial confusion, by *lawful*, Miller means responsive to reasons and the process of reasoning. Because the process of reasoning about the best ways of living, or the best forms of education, transforms the types of questions we ask and the types of reasons we give in the process of answering those questions, we can see the pursuit of lawfulness as dynamic. For example, when we study a subject like moral philosophy, our understanding of the moral landscape expands. Instead of seeing moral life in narrow terms—follow a set of rules, follow the dictates of one's family or one's religion—disinterested study introduces us to the great variety of experiments in living that moral philosophy has provoked. We begin to see that moral philosophy doesn't provide us with an easy answer to the simplistic questions we brought with us to college. Instead, it invites us into conversation with "the minds which possessed the vigor and tension" representative of lawful thinking; that is, thinking responsive to reasons, not mere conformity to simplistic rules or the dictates of tradition.

A liberal education causes us to admire those vigorous minds capable of holding together the greatest tension, and it "promises association with those creative minds." This is a clear advance beyond the platitude that liberal education makes a student well-rounded. Liberal education confers power on anyone who exerts vigor to bring competing ideas together. To take one example from my own teaching, in my course on educational policy, students want to know if charter schools are good or bad. They expect someone who is smart enough to be a professor to also be smart enough to provide the types of answers that are in opinion pages and on cable news. Instead of offering ready answers, the liberal study of educational policy offers students the opportunity to ask questions like: What does it mean to call a school successful? How would we know if a charter school were successful? More, it asks students to study the history of charter schools. Students are surprised to learn that charter schools weren't opened in opposition to public schools, but as a way to reform public schools from the inside. Finally, students are reminded that good and bad results from some charter schools may not say anything significant about all charter schools. The liberal study of educational policy complicates easy solutions, building tension in those who study, so that when they do propose a solution or weigh in on a debate they do so with vigor, inoculated against the types of fads and rhetoric that seek to flatten the complex art of educating into prices that can be manipulated. Though the liberally educated may not appear as powerful as someone who offers immediate answers and easy solutions, Miller wants us to appreciate the type of power liberal education makes possible. Students of the liberal arts aren't afraid of hard problems and complex thinking. They act in the face of these difficulties, and they seek the company of thinkers, alive and dead, who've also harnessed tensions that result in creative power.[80]

The desire to keep company with those who've earned the creative power that comes with being liberally educated is the reason why Miller can assert that liberal education "lives chiefly in its exemplars." Something a great book's approach, or an approach to liberal education centered around curriculum, can miss is the significance of creative power exercised by individual men and women. Emerson understood the importance of highlighting the potential of the individual thinker, because he hoped to inspire young people to exercise their birthright as individuals capable of thought. One needn't be perfect or fully formed in order to take part in important conversations on how to live well. And, one doesn't need to go back to the works of the past in order to find answers to the problems we are confronting today. As Emerson notes, we go back to the works of the past to get in touch with the energy that inspired men and women to think boldly and act creatively.[81] It is that energy—that morale, that vigor—that is important, and liberal education keeps that energy alive by showing how it can be an active force in the lives of students today. Miller demonstrates his full appreciation of this point when he writes, "Good men, and great men, have been degraded because they have been presented as more logical, more shrewd, or more informed rather than as free and self-contained spirits whose adventurous temper we need to make our own."

We *degrade* the great books when we make it seem as if the men and women who wrote them were something like careerists who had a knack for producing masterpieces. Instead, we should see thinking as the powerful and passionate act it is. Men and women devoted to thinking are "free and self-contained spirits" who have an "adventurous temper we need to make our own." There are two points worth stressing here. Powerful thinkers are free *and* self-contained. A mistake that Emerson himself seems to invite is that taking license, or freedom from any restraint, is the same thing as creative power. Energy that is not channeled into a meaningful purpose often dissipates. By contrast, disciplined energy is power. The person who is free and self-contained accepts great discipline, but only a discipline that offers the promise of advancing what they take to be their mission or purpose. As discussed earlier in this section, liberal education cannot be equated with consumerism, because the incoming student doesn't know what to hope for. Over the process of coming into contact with free and self-contained spirits through their liberal education, the student learns what their hopes are and accepts those disciplines that promise to develop that hope into creative power. This leads to Miller's second point: liberal education is an adventure.[82] The disciplined energy we experience when engaging with exemplars of liberal education also teaches us to make their adventurous temper our own.

But so much conspires against making our education an adventure. We know how expensive a college education is, we know how important it is to find a job after graduation, we know that the guarantees of vocational and more practical paths have their attractions, and we know that the expert who offers answers where the liberally educated ask questions is often given more respect and prestige. Our creative power can look pale in comparison to their accredited power. Still, Miller encourages us to take heart, reminding us of the exemplars who gave themselves over to the adventures of thinking in the face of their doubts and in the face of their own doubters. Though the thinker may not experience success in their own time, their creative power often bends the arc of the moral universe to the good. Socrates was killed, but he remains a powerful provocation for anyone seeking to make the world better. As Miller reminds us in section four: "Liberal education can make men; it cannot promise to make them rich, powerful, honored or happy." Engaging with exemplars of the liberally educated, we feel the choice between creative power that speaks to our higher ideals and power that cheapens our dignity to a mere price. Our society sends the very loud message—choose the easy power, choose money and success—but liberal education offers the quiet but firm invitation: you know where the easy path leads, why not risk the adventure of becoming a person you can, on reflection, be proud of? It doesn't tell us what that person is; instead, it invites us into the mystery of figuring that out, using the best thinking we can muster in the process.[83]

§

Section 5 calls us to consider the connection between mystery and adventure. The type of adventure Miller advocates is not the destructive drive to conquer or destroy. Rather, the adventure of liberal education is in accepting the invitation to live meaningful questions, trusting that the process of asking hard questions will result in creative power. The term *mastery learning* is gaining traction in educational conversations, but Miller is right to remind us that liberal learning is often more about mystery than mastery. Here is how he puts it: "The liberal man, like the religious man, can believe only where there is mystery. Foolish men confound mystery with obscurantism, whereas mystery is rather promise, and the unfolding of promise into new revelation and new powers."

If there was no mystery, belief would be unnecessary. Belief only flourishes in the face of an authentic mystery. For a student undergoing a liberal education, there is often no greater mystery than the question: Who am I? Liberal education doesn't dispel the mystery with the simple answer: You are a future doctor, or, You are a partisan in a religious or political debate, or, You are a consumer. At the same time, Miller is also right to remind us that mystery is not obscurantism: the pedantic professor holding himself above students and the world in his brilliance, cultivating initiates instead of independent thinkers. Rather, the greatest mysteries are often ready-to-hand, hidden in plain sight.[84] What does it mean to be a good parent, a good neighbor, a responsible steward of priceless values? Asking these questions and not accepting simple answers invites us into conversations that have been ongoing since we've had language, reminding us that there will never be a time when the meaning of being human will not be a question for us.[85]

Living these questions is not withdrawing from our shared social world into an ivory tower or the private language of the initiated. Rather, we learn to ask difficult questions so that we make good on the promise of "new revelation and new powers." At the risk of digressing, I find it notable that one of the most celebrated social reformers in education, Geoffrey Canada, graduated from Bowdoin College. Though we may disagree about the long-term significance of the Harlem Children's Zone, I don't think we can downplay the ways in which Canada exercised real vision and real creative power to the betterment of individual children who experienced what Canada built.[86] Similarly, one of our most important contemporary civil rights activists, DeRay Mckesson, also attended Bowdoin

College, and credits his education with helping him develop the type of creative hope and vision that we need now more than ever.[87] Both men experienced disinterested study that empowered them to ask new questions and seek new solutions to real problems in the world. This is something Miller trusts and asks us to believe in. Though there is pressure to dispel mystery in the name of practical results, Miller believes that trusting in mystery may, in the long run, be far more efficacious than seeking shortcuts to mastery.

§

The pressures of credentialism can keep students from trusting in liberal education. How can we make liberal education more of an invitation to an adventure? How can we show students the good of an adventure that brings them into the presence of the mystery of their own purpose and their own worth? These are the questions that Miller thinks we need to ask ourselves. Credentialism brings a weariness to study and the life of liberal education, where mystery inspires revelation. When we trust liberal education, new opportunities and new values are revealed. To take a common experience my students share with me: they register for a class because it fulfills a graduation requirement, but they end the semester transformed. The required course makes it so that they can't help but see the world and their place in it differently. A course that seemed a mere formality ended up containing passion and great intellect that are exemplary of a way of thinking they can aspire to. Liberal education routinely frees the creative power of students, and Miller asks that we consider what happens when we make this fact central to the work of our teaching and the way we think about liberal education.

SECTIONS 6 AND 11: ILLIBERAL LIBERAL ARTS

Section six is brief, direct, and largely critical. Miller warns that liberal arts institutions can be illiberal, and that saving a liberal arts college does not mean saving liberal education. Section II develops these thoughts, but before turning to section II, it is worth dwelling on some of the dangers of illiberality that liberal arts colleges face.

A major reason a liberal arts college will fall into illiberality is due to lack of trust. Instead of trusting the good of liberal education, trusting that students and teachers working together in small classes on important texts and ideas will be beneficial, we seek shortcuts. Fads are introduced, new majors and minors are piloted, and resources are diverted outside of the classroom into new ventures. For example, countless scholars have lamented the rise of the administrative class on college campuses.[88] With the increase of administrators comes the emergence of groups catering to the needs of administrators: consultants, data analysts, financial planners specializing in higher education, etc. Though there is likely a need for professionals on college campuses focused on aspects of the institution that are not classroom or learning-focused, the balance today can feel off. It can come to seem like administrators and consultants at liberal arts colleges do not understand liberal education, and this is having an illiberal effect on the life of campus culture.[89] It is demoralizing to think that the mission of a college can be set by a marketing firm, and it is insulting to think that presence is being traded for promises of technology-mediated personalized learning and efficiency models that relegate the moral heart of teaching to a quaint vestige of times past. Much more could be said on this point, but as Miller dwelled briefly on the negative, so will I.

Related to the rise of the administrative class is the rising importance of athletics on college campuses.[90] There is good scholarship on this topic, but I turn to two exemplary college presidents to make this point. Alexander Meiklejohn, president of Amherst College from 1912 to 1924, warned about the dangers of college athletics. He resisted the call to hire coaches for college sports and resisted the drive to charge money for college athletic contests.[91] He thought both moves would undermine the liberal purposes of the college, and we have to wonder if he was correct in his concern. While president of Yale in the 1980s, A. Bartlett Giamatti issued a dire warning about how athletics were harming liberal education.[92] Giamatti, who became the commissioner of Major League Baseball, was very clearly not anti-sport. But he did have the courage to ask other college presidents to consider the risks to liberal learning when sports came to dominate a student's schedule. Though the place of athletics at elite liberal colleges seems untouchable, it is worth wondering about their role in facilitating liberal learning and then wondering what it would take to make sure that sports lived up to the platitudes asserted in their promotional material. Though it is believable that sports can build character, it is harder to believe that a coach would choose starters based on the level of character they demonstrated or developed because of athletics over someone who was simply a good athlete.[93] Again, I don't want to dwell on the negative, but we must ask if the balance is off when it comes to athletics actually promoting liberal education. Sports can be a great thing, but they should not be the center of a student's life at a liberal arts college.[94]

Finally, just as the role of sports is unquestioned at liberal arts colleges, the image of the liberal arts college as a sort of Club Med for the young is also hard to question. Colleges compete to provide students with the best amenities, which is not bad in itself. But when the social life of college is almost completely unmoored from its educational mission, it is worth asking difficult questions. Leon Botstein, president of Bard College, noted, "A college ought to be measured by the extent to which the curriculum influences dining hall conversation and the kinds of entertainment students choose."[95] If this sentiment sounds nostalgic or unrealistic, I think it says more about our cynicism than it does about Botstein's thinking. If we believe that a liberal education makes a student a lifelong learner or a lifelong representative of the liberally educated person, shouldn't we be more concerned about the quality of student conversation and choice in entertainment than we are with making sure the college has the fastest internet so that students can stream whatever, and how much, media they care to consume?

§

The problem with taking Botstein's statement seriously is that it runs us into the other direction illiberality can take. That is, a liberally educated person is not someone who only reads great books or who only watches serious film. A philosopher like Ted Cohen can facilitate more thinking with so-called low art than most critics can hope to get from a lifetime engaged with serious art.[96] It is not Botstein's point to mandate certain objects of attention; it is to remind us that liberal colleges should care, more than they seem to do now, about the quality of attention students bring to their experiences outside of the classroom. We should care, because we hope that a student's liberal education will inform how they live. I agree with Botstein, but I also agree with Miller's concern, expressed forcefully in section II, that a professor must be very careful about unduly influencing a student's taste in art or beliefs in politics, religion, or morality. Though we want a student to take up the work of self-education outside of the classroom, it is good to worry about the risks of our influence and appreciate that a successful liberal education is not the same as a student attaching themselves to liberal causes or ideas.

In a way, the point is an obvious one, though you wouldn't know it if you were watching cable news. Liberal arts colleges are not indoctrination centers. There is no party line that students must adhere to, and though some faculty members at liberal arts colleges have very progressive views, college trustees and institutional policies are generally conservative in the best sense of the word. Though some individual faculty may go too far in pushing a left-leaning view of the world, the majority of college professors respect their students far too much to tell them what or how to think. I know there is no hope in convincing the true believer that liberal arts colleges are not deeply illiberal indoctrination centers, so I won't try. But for someone who is worried about professors inadvertently pushing their views on a college student, Miller's thinking in section II is very helpful.

The section begins: "The liberal teacher must take care to present only as much as the student can appropriate in his will and understanding." Here, I think again of the role of presence in teaching. A professor is not teaching anyone in any place; they teach particular students at a particular point in their development. It can be hard for someone who teaches their favorite author every semester to appreciate that a student may struggle to understand what they are experiencing for the first time, but this is a key marker of being present with students. We must anticipate their frustrations, celebrate their insights, and find a way to make the material appropriately challenging. If we don't do this, students may resort to guessing what it is they think we, their professors, believe or want students to believe. Instead of doing the work of thinking for themselves, they attempt to divine where we stand, and pitch their remarks or writing to what they think we want to hear. The result is disappointing. Students don't experience the adventure of thinking, and professors don't learn much about who their students are and what they actually care about. Presence disappears as students seek conformity to what they take their professor's views to be.

Miller goes on, addressing the inexperienced teacher who thinks that they are reaching students without realizing they are only reaching students at the level of surface thinking. He writes, "The average undergraduate creates the illusion of liberal advance because his intelligence permits facility in memory work. Yet he may have understood very little. Especially is this appearance of liberalism likely to result when the materials studied seems by itself to guarantee an emancipated mind." The movie *The Squid and the Whale* is a crushing portrait of a pretentious college professor and his son who tries desperately to impress him. At one point in the movie, the son—trying to impress a young woman—talks about

Franz Kafka's work. Intrigued, the woman asks the son what he likes about Kafka's work. All the son can say is that the work is very Kafkaesque. This is a perfect parody of what Miller is directing our attention to. Students can be quite adept at appearing as if they are moved by their liberal education, but they may be merely parroting slogans: they haven't understood the foundation of their beliefs.

This may be especially the case when students are doing the type of thinking we would categorize as liberal. Though the professor is not pushing an agenda on the student, they may be particularly apt to let a student's viewpoint stand unchallenged if it is progressive or left-leaning. For example, a professor may know it is important to challenge a student's unblinking adherence to a religious tradition, but they may not feel it is as necessary to challenge a student's critique of the patriarchy, thinking a student's willingness to offer this critique is a marker that they are becoming liberally educated. Miller wants us to take this point very seriously, and he writes, "No one has a liberal education because he has studied "liberal" rather than "illiberal" doctrines or movements. Because many do not make this distinction our liberals are so often unapproachable in their dogmatism." These are strong words, and worth considering. The criticism often leveled against liberal arts colleges by conservative thinkers is that they don't offer balance. Though the critic who levies this charge would never think for a moment that syllabi must be balanced in other ways—balanced in terms of gender, balanced in terms of race, balanced in terms of sexuality of the authors on the syllabus—the idea that a syllabus must have an equal number of conservative and liberal thinkers is taken to be not only reasonable, but a strong argument for the illiberality of liberal arts colleges.[97]

We have to see the limitations of this argument. As a professional educator, the college professor is responsible for bringing the best work to their students. A student doesn't deserve a balance of authors in a literature course; instead, a student should experience the best authors for that particular literature course.

Of course, it is always an open debate why a work should be considered the best, or excellent, and this is where liberal education comes in. Students are taught to understand and appreciate the work under discussion, so that when it comes time to talk about an author like Kafka, they can say more than "Kafka is excellent because he is so Kafkaesque." It is not enough that students can repeat the right things about literature: *x* is a good author, *y* is a good book, but they must understand why this is the case. The same holds for political, moral, and religious beliefs. It is not enough to hold a view; one must understand why the view makes sense, and especially why the view makes sense to the person holding it. It is very possible to hold liberal views illiberally. Someone who is raised in a liberal household but doesn't understand where their beliefs come from or why they matter or how they differ from the alternative views is no more liberally educated than the student from a conservative or a religious home who hasn't critically examined their views.

Changing direction slightly, it is important to appreciate that just as no amount of repeating certain phrases will make a student liberally educated, a student who doesn't yet know what they believe about a book or a political issue is not irredeemable. I find this is much more of a peer-to-peer issue but one that impacts the life of classrooms nonetheless. A student who hasn't learned how to think or talk about transgender rights may say something that their peers find offensive. It is often easier to police the student's language than it is to facilitate learning for that student. It is certainly not the job of the offended student to offer that education, but the policing of a student's language can make it more difficult for the student to learn in a way that would allow them to *understand* why their speech is found offensive. To be clear, I am not defending offensive speech for its educational value.[98] What I am asserting is that policing offensive speech is not the same thing as educating a student so that they fully understand why their speech is found to be offensive while also offering them the opportunity to reconsider how they speak and what they believe. More, just because a student is capable of policing speech does not automatically mean that they also understand the grounds for their beliefs. If we care about liberal education, and not just helping students repeat things that sound like what a liberally educated person might say, we have to make sure that students are exercising the creative power of thought. This is made difficult if we don't "take care to present only as much as the student can appropriate in his will and understanding." We have to get to know our students well enough, through their reflection papers and seminar-style discussions, that we understand how they hold their beliefs. Then we can learn how to teach so that they feel confident enough to question those beliefs.

This is a point worth stressing. Another criticism commonly levied by conservatives against liberal arts students is that they are snowflakes.[99] This view is harmful on many levels, but it is most harmful at the level of helping a student understand their beliefs. The idea of creating a safe space in the classroom is not tantamount to letting students avoid the difficulties of thinking.[100] Rather, a safe space—at least as I understand it—is a space where we create conditions that allow students the freedom to think. If students feel threatened or under attack, they may merely react defensively or completely shut down. Neither response is educative. Students need to be given whatever support they need to process difficult topics. Doing this is not catering to their "snowflake nature"; it just makes good pedagogic sense. A good teacher reaches a student where they are, not so that the student stays at that stage of development, but so that the teacher is sure the student is thinking and not just repeating a phrase that will make the teacher feel as if they are doing their job. Miller makes this point in a very helpful way: "Nothing is liberal in effect unless it can become a calm possession of a confident mind. . . . In sum, it is dangerous to carry the humanities beyond the point where their content loses meaning in the actually established values of the student."

Both points are worth stressing. First, the result of a liberal education is a confident mind that calmly possesses its values. The liberally educated person is not violent or defensive, but this doesn't mean that they aren't committed, devoted, dedicated. Rather, because the liberally educated person has subjected their beliefs and values to self-criticism, new ideas aren't seen as threats, they are seen as opportunities to enlarge thinking. One of the many problems caused by social media is that we are encouraged to think in terms of immediacy. We are bombarded with news and information and we feel compelled to react to every passing item. It is easy to bring this mindset into the classroom. Instead of seeing a student's life as unfolding over time, we may feel pressure to have them express an opinion *now*, worried that if we don't reach the student now, all is lost. One of the main problems with this mindset is that our feelings of immediacy don't always line up with the "actually established values of the student." The world of the student may have very different concerns in its present orbit, and the urgency we feel may leave little impact on him or her. Worse, it may be alienating.

As difficult as it can feel, we need to be present with students where they are. Though our world is full of urgencies that we feel called to respond to in the moment, we have to be *with* the student, appreciating what they are concerned about and interested in. More, though we know we only have a limited amount of time with each student—a semester, a year, four years—we can't let this throw us out of our own confident mind that calmly possesses its values. A student may not remember many of the things we tell them years after they graduate, but they will remember our presence and the presence we created in the classroom. Though there is immediate satisfaction in assertive thinking—winning a debate, stating our position in a way that leads to immediate assent from our audience—there are already countless outlets for this type of thinking. The calm possession of a confident mind has very few havens left outside of the liberal arts college, and we should appreciate the power in that. Our students don't need us to be a pundit, they don't need us to be clever, they don't need us to tell them that the world is falling apart around them. They get this all the time. What students crave is someone with real confidence who holds values with the tenderness that they deserve.

Society seems convinced that this type of tenderness, one that cultivates value quietly but firmly, is a sign of weakness. But liberal education, if we trust it, has its own creative power. It doesn't need to be loud and illiberal. The students who come to us are wonderful, and we need to trust that as well. Though they may not say wise or fully-informed things at first or all the time, though they may need a great deal of support to gain a confident mind, if we trust their capacities for thinking, if we address their actually established values with respect, they learn how to exercise creative power. If we do our jobs well, they will question us, and they will question our beliefs. This may not seem like power, but it is. Students will look to us as exemplars of the calm and confident mind, and this will have a lasting impact on their lives. A professor doesn't proffer secrets to the initiated—they give students the gift of confidence that allows them to be self-critical and self-possessed. It frees them to establish their own presence, and there is no greater marker of our success as liberal educators than having a hand in helping a student establish their presence in the world.

This is not to downplay all the ways liberal education is under attack or all of the important issues that are indeed pressing down on us. But even as we acknowledge these pressures, it is important that we aren't thrown off our axis, keeping us from doing what is within our power every day in our respective classrooms. We can be exemplars of the liberally educated mind, and we can free students to take possession of their own mind, forming their values through self-criticism and commitment.

Though these sections started on a negative note, thinking through the differences between liberal and illiberal education is ultimately useful in helping us appreciate why liberal education, and the presence of its representatives, remains the quietly powerful force it is. It may not directly solve the problems facing it and our wider society, but I trust that the presence of more liberally educated people will ultimately have positive effects if we have the courage to continue trusting in it.

SECTION 7: MORALE

John William Miller's address to graduating students at Hobart College focused on the importance of morale. A liberal education can strengthen student morale, so that those students might persist in the face of conflicts that will inevitably arise over the course of their lives. In section 7 Miller focuses on the importance of the teacher's morale. This topic remains a timely one, for some of the reasons mentioned in the previous section. Though liberal arts colleges, in general, remain committed to tenure, and tenured faculty do most of the teaching on campus, decisions that are centrally important to their work are increasingly being made by administrators and consultants. Though professors have academic freedom when it comes to what they teach, colleges routinely decide what majors should be offered and this leaves humanities majors and courses vulnerable to being cut in favor of more marketable offerings.[101] As I make clear earlier in this book, I am not opposed to any major being added to a liberal arts curriculum on principle. But I am deeply opposed to any decision that relegates the centrality of presence in a liberal arts education to the margins of discussions about the curriculum or the mission of liberal education.

Philosopher of education Doris Santoro has developed a groundbreaking line of research around teacher demoralization.[102] Santoro argues that demoralization is different from burnout, because a teacher experiences demoralization when they feel that they cannot do the type of teaching that is professionally responsible given their understanding of teaching as a moral act. This happens, for example, when teachers have to read from scripted curriculum, or when they have to devote more time to test preparation than experiential learning, or when the measure of their worth as a teacher is taken by student results on standardized assessments. You can add to this the low pay and countless insults from conservative politicians that have real consequences in terms of the ability of teacher unions to organize, and we can see why there is a resurgence of teacher-strikes and calls from the public to stop attacking teachers. Though the situation faced by public school teachers is different in many ways from that faced by professors at liberal arts colleges, there is a risk of demoralization when we lose touch with the moral heart of teaching at the college level. Section 7 is Miller's attempt to draw us back to this moral center, and we can use this center to develop the morale we will need to wrest the vision that drives liberal colleges and liberal education away from consultants and administrators who, in the worst cases, see these small colleges as steps up the ladder to higher-paid administrative positions or just another consulting gig.

This may be too harsh, but I am not always sure. Miller begins section 7 with the line: "A proper conception of the liberal education is of first importance to teachers, and to their morale." If we valued liberal education in the ways we should, then everyone associated with liberal education would make it their mission to develop a proper conception of liberal education, knowing that this is not something that can be delivered via PowerPoint and in an afternoon. There would be book studies about the liberal arts, and every new employee at a liberal arts college, especially faculty and administrators, would devote significant time to studying liberal education. I don't have the power to mandate this vision into reality, but what I hope to do in the rest of this section is to spend some time thinking through what a proper conception of liberal education might look like, as a way of providing one entryway into a conversation I hope happens more widely than it does. A proper conception of liberal education would immediately build faculty morale, and this, in turn, would make the college a more inviting place for students. This, not what is for sale from educational consultants, is what we should be devoting our attention to, and Miller's essay helps us appreciate why this is the case.

§

"A proper conception of the liberal education is of first importance to teachers, and to their morale." What Miller reminds us of in this line is that teaching at a liberal arts college remains a line of work that can become a vocation. We can draw deep strength from knowing that we are doing important work, work that has value in a world where everything can be monetized. When we have a better understanding of the importance and potential of our work, we experience morale, because we can persist in the face of the inevitable challenges and setbacks we will face. These setbacks, if they are persistent enough, can lead to deep frustration, but if we are mindful of Santoro's thinking on demoralization, then we can resist demoralization by making sure our work is animated by the moral resources that remain available whenever a teacher is fully present with students.

Miller doesn't offer a simplistic or naïve hope, but it is one that can animate the ways we conceive of our calling as teachers. He writes, "The teachers of the liberal arts know that they have nothing to offer except the intrinsic worth of critical adventure." Weighed in the balance, this may not seem like a lot. Instead of making broad claims for the importance of liberal education, he tells teachers that they have nothing to offer, except, of course, "the intrinsic worth of critical adventure." So much is packed into this line. To begin, Miller reminds professors that their work has intrinsic worth. It is tempting for us to commodify our time, weighing the costs of spending extra time in office hours against the benefits of doing more of our own research, but Miller reminds us that we get to do work that has intrinsic worth in office hours and through our research. Giving a young person the gift of self-confident thinking is beyond price. It may not always feel that way, pulled as we are between so many competing demands, but we cannot forget that teaching remains a vocation in touch with deep sources of intrinsic worth.

Interestingly, this deep source of worth lies in nothing more, though nothing less, than allowing students the experience of "critical adventure." This way of putting it captures the sense that liberal education teaches students to be self-critical, but for the purpose of discovering something of deep personal significance. Liberal thinking is not cynical, it does not destroy for the sake of the feeling of power that comes with destruction. Rather, liberal education is critical in the way that a gardener uses pruning shears is. We cut away misconceptions and growths down wrong paths so that we might shape and cultivate something of worth. Of course, we can always go wrong, but that is why liberal education is an adventure. It is up to us to take responsibility for the direction our thinking and self-development will take, and the best our guides can do is offer morale: they cannot answer the questions for us. Miller writes, "There is no particular good to be derived from Plato, or Shakespeare, or Emerson, or Einstein. These are disinterested minds and their meaning is lost in so far as one is not prepared to walk in their steps, however remotely."

Two points are worth stressing here in relation to a teacher's morale. First, though Miller uses the negative "no particular good," he does so to clarify the positive good of liberal education. Though we can't determine with certainty or in advance what a student will get from engaging with Emerson or Shakespeare, we can take heart trusting that having students engage with these thinkers—walking in their steps, however remotely—will help students experience the critical adventure of disinterested thought. Though we cannot offer easily marketable guarantees from this experience, we offer students something more: the chance to take control of thinking about their life and its purpose. Liberal education demands that students take ownership of their thinking, and there is no better way to facilitate this than by getting students in the company of thinkers who have claimed responsibility for their educations. A teacher can develop morale from putting students in this company of thinkers. One of the greatest compliments I can get as a teacher is when a student tells me that a book we've discussed has touched them in some way and that this one book opened a path to a new line of interest. I don't want students who think like me, but I do want students who find something in my courses that moves them to take up the adventure of self-education.

Second, just as we can draw morale from the introductions we make for our students, we should remember that our work allows us the freedom to walk in the same footsteps we free our students to walk in. In a way, the point goes without saying, but at those times in the year where we feel burdened with the daily demands of our work, we can forget how lucky we are to be in a world of value, often one of our free choosing. I value reading someone like James Baldwin, always finding a new lens to exercise self-criticism and love through his writing,[103] and I shouldn't forget that as a professor I get paid to read and teach Baldwin. I am compensated for something that brings value into my life, both through the work my students do and through the work that I get to do. Just as I worry I may have been too harsh in my criticism of administrators and consultants in the previous section, I worry here that I will be taken to be overly sentimental about the work of teaching. Acknowledging this risk, I stand by the importance of recognizing the sources of value that are only available to us liberal educators, defending them when they are under attack and drawing morale and sustenance from them when I feel demoralized. A proper conception of the liberal arts, one that teaches us that this form of education can free a student to take control of their education, opening them to a world of value they've never experienced, is deeply important for our morale.

I can only hope that more faculty advocate for conversations that build morale and that administrators realize that giving "the impression that a college exists for any purpose of a special sort" untethered from the intrinsic value of the critical adventure of self-education undercuts the morale that is freely available and always present when teachers and students work together in moral seriousness, walking in the steps of the liberally educated. The next section develops this thinking through a deeper consideration of what terms like self-education mean for liberal education.

SECTION 8: FATEFUL EXPERIENCES

Section 8 begins on what feels like a solipsistic or even an illiberal note. Miller writes that "there is no point of view not defined by the liberal attitude which can recommend the liberal education." The idea here seems to be that someone who isn't already committed to liberal education cannot be brought to see the value of liberal education. As such, there is no way to *argue* anyone into seeing the point of liberal education, because liberal education has to be experienced to be valued.[104]

While this can be a closed stance, Miller means something invitational, even expansive, by suggesting that argument is not the way into valuing liberal education. One way of understanding what Miller means here is through the work of William James, another influence on Miller. In his lovely series of lectures collected under the title *Talks to Students on Some of Life's Ideals*, James discusses the importance of feeling the joy of passionate pursuit of some good. In the final lecture, "What Makes a Life Significant," James writes:

> Every Jack sees in his own particular Jill charms and perfections to the enchantment of which we stolid onlookers are stone-cold. And which has the superior view of the absolute truth, he or we? Which has the more vital insight into the nature of Jill's existence, as a fact? Is he in excess, being in this matter a maniac? or are we in defect, being victims of a pathological anesthesia as regards Jill's magical importance?

> Surely the latter; surely to Jack are the profounder truths revealed.[105]

James is getting at a very important point here: The engaged standpoint offers an experience of the world that is inaccessible to the detached observer.[106] Though impartiality is often taken to be the hallmark of good scientific research, James reminds his audience of college students that there are many truths in the world that are only available through partiality. The lover, in this case Jack, knows more—and often knows better—about Jill than someone who studies her dispassionately.

Miller is getting at something similar in his thinking about liberal education. Someone dispassionately examining liberal education may completely miss the adventure, whereas someone who has committed a life to it will have access to a world of sustaining value. This does not mean that one must undergo something like a conversion experience or exercise blind faith in liberal education in order to appreciate its value. But it does mean that liberal education will not disclose its value to anyone who is not willing to undergo the rigors of liberal education. Here again we see the role that trust plays in liberal education. To get the benefits of liberal education we must freely choose to trust that this form of education will be worth our investment. We cannot be argued into this choice or this investment; trust and aspiration seem better ways of describing the first stages of liberal education.

Here, too, is where we see how the charge that liberal education is itself a form of indoctrination loses its force. At each stage of the process, the student is freely investing their attention in order to discover what they can learn from the process of becoming liberally educated. Because it is not something that they were argued into, a promissory note that they expect to be paid out at the end of the experience, they are largely responsible for the direction that the education will take. As such, "this outcome"—the realization that liberal education is not something that can be valued outside of the process of undergoing the education—"has a great use, namely to make plain what was above suggested; that at the last one confronts men and not ideas, and that the authority of various views develops freely from the pattern of a personal integrity and power. Consequently, one must go one's way. This is the residual risk of the liberal."

There is so much packed into these few short sentences, as Miller condenses many of the key insights from sections 1 to 7 into them. Here, again, Miller reminds us that the end of a liberal education is the formation of character. We don't confront mere ideas through liberal education; we test the quality of the person who was capable of the thinking and we, in turn, consider what type of person we hope to become through the process of becoming educated. Taking responsibility for our aspirations, we come to realize the ways in which the quality of our thinking determines our integrity and power. If we don't care about our thought, through cynicism or indifference or opportunism, our integrity suffers. More, someone who is liberally educated can *read* this about us and other people. In our interactions with others, it is not just the ideas that are being taken stock of, because in human interactions "one confronts men and not ideas." Hence the significance of presence. When we are in the presence of someone who has integrity it is immediately felt. A corollary of this realization is that no one can do our thinking for us, because the quality of our thinking shows up in our very presence. We are responsible for the presence we make manifest, and "consequently, one must go one's way." A liberal education is most certainly not indoctrination, because its ideal outcome is one where a student goes their own way, for better and worse. "This is the residual risk of the liberal." Unlike forms of education that are not liberal, we are not guaranteed an outcome. A vocational teacher fails if their student cannot pick up the trade, just as a guru fails if they don't win an acolyte. The liberal educator, by contrast, fails only when the student is unwilling, or is unprepared, to take up the work of going their own way. But the way the student goes is something up to the liberally educated, not the liberal educator.

§

If this were the whole truth, the liberal educator could reasonably be charged with disingenuousness. After all, and of course, we want our students to make wise decisions that lead to more humane forms of living. The risk of letting the student go their own way is guided by trust that the student will be positively impacted by liberal education. Importantly, Miller continues his thinking: "This is the residual risk of the liberal. But the hope of eventual agreement lies precisely in the sort of fateful experiences which the disinterested mind invites. The practice of freedom can alone disclose its form and its laws." Again, there is so much distillation of thought captured in three short sentences, and again Miller offers a profoundly moving vision of the enduring good of liberal education. The idea that learning is a "fateful experience," where we trust our own freedom enough to hope that the process of liberal education will bring us into eventual agreement, is awe inspiring.[107] The disinterested mind is unafraid of self-reliance: it freely follows an idea wherever it leads. Instead of fearing that free inquiry will prove alienating, there is a hope that the honest pursuit of the true and the good will ultimately lead to the creation of eventual agreement with others similarly engaged in free and honest inquiry. But we can never be assured of this in advance, and so we must trust that freely and disinterestedly following an idea with integrity will usher in a higher and more authentic form of community.[108]

Each person pursuing a liberal education, and professors are also always engaged in this process, runs "the residual risk of the liberal," which is the risk of taking responsibility for discovering who they are and who they should become, what they believe, and what they should believe. If we knew any of these things in advance of inquiry, there would be no need for education: indoctrination would suffice. But because the world is always changing, and because we change the more we understand our self and our world, the process is always—as Miller stresses in section 5—a dynamic one that cannot be controlled in advance of inquiry. We go into study with this disinterested spirit, knowing that "the practice of freedom can alone disclose its form and its laws."

Liberal education is this practice of freedom, where we find out what it means to trust ourselves with free inquiry into matters of the utmost importance. From the outside, hemmed in by fears and assumptions about a way of life we haven't yet experienced, the world of liberal education is opaque and bound to be misunderstood and misrepresented. Only someone with an adventurous spirit who is able to discover the form and the laws of freedom will learn the value of liberal education. This means a student must be willing to risk free inquiry, not knowing with certainty where it will lead but trusting that it will be better than conformity and the limitations of established modes of thinking, believing, and self. Though the known is comforting, once we know something to be mediocre and limiting, or just plain false, we are positioned to run the risk of freedom. The risk of the educational unknown is worth taking in the face of the certainty of mediocrity or falsehood should we not choose freedom.

The adventure of freedom is ongoing and so we are always working to discover its form and laws. This is one of the main reasons why liberal education remains deeply important. As we make scientific and technological advances, we will be challenged more than ever to keep pace in terms of how we understand our self and our place in the world.[109] Liberal education doesn't provide ready answers, but it keeps the adventure alive and the hope that the process of free inquiry will lead to stronger bonds of agreement and community than through enforced conformity. This aspect of liberal education is difficult, if not impossible, to appreciate from the outside, because it can feel as if the only way to come into agreement is by tabling the possibility of disagreement through conformity. Taking up the risk of the self-criticism called for by free inquiry seems to consign us to conflict and division. But Miller reminds us of the importance of showing students that free inquiry can lead to deep agreement, but to get to this agreement we need to discover the laws and the form of freedom that make this agreement possible, something that only happens when someone is empowered with the morale necessary to undertake a liberal education. Section 10 develops this thinking in more detail, discussing the ways that the fateful experience of freedom can lead to the development of community.

SECTION 9: DELIVERING THE CURRICULUM

In section 9, Miller moves his reader from the height of viewing liberal education as a fateful experience of freedom down to practical matters related to teaching methods and the curriculum. This section doesn't exhibit the same composed concision of many of the others, but two main themes emerge: avoiding undue optimism, and the role that character plays in delivering a liberal education.

§

"Administrators sometimes exhibit undue optimism" when it comes to new models and methods of teaching or curricular innovation. While Miller understands that change is necessary—citing, as an example, the plan of study at the University of Michigan—he is also wary of the pursuit of "curricular utopia."[110]

With the passage of time, I worry we've only become more willing to embrace the "undue optimism" Miller warns of. To take an obvious example, technology and the edupreneurial industry have offered themselves as routes to educational improvement. Everything from massive open online courses to personalized learning playlists are being heralded and piloted.[111] Significant, for me, are the emerging reports that the very people making these technologies are fighting hard to keep their children as far away from them as possible.[112] As Waldorf Education grows in Silicon Valley, parents and educators across America are being sold technology as the solution to countless educational problems.[113] If a person says they have a product that will save a child that they aren't giving to their own children, then this, alone, should give one reason to pause.[114] But more to the point, Miller is on target when he reminds us that there is no positive solution when it comes to helping a student become liberally educated. The best we can do is "remove the hindrances to the attainment of liberal outlooks." And, unfortunately for the technologist and the edupreneur, there are no shortcuts here. A student must trust in their ability to ask very hard questions that matter deeply to them, and they must be around other people similarly engaged in asking these questions. Classroom discussion, conversations during office hours, being in the presence of men and women further along in the process of becoming liberally educated: these are the ways that we put a student in the position to attain a liberal education.

Here, too, we can see why liberal education is not tantamount to liberal indoctrination. Liberal education does not walk a student through their paces, knowing in advance where the education will lead and choosing techniques that will most successfully get a student there. Rather, "one must proceed . . . by discovering hindrances to freedom." Here, the liberal college exhibits its conservative tendencies. A liberal arts college doesn't embrace the next educational fad, it trusts in its long history of putting a student in the position of exploring their freedom. Anything that gets in the way of pursuing this freedom should be avoided, and positive suggestions for how this process can be speeded along or made more efficient must be looked at with a great degree of skepticism if not outright derision. As Miller reminds us in the section immediately preceding this one, the fateful experience of freedom is the hallmark of liberal education, and anything that gets in the way of helping a student experience this, no matter the sales pitch, should be cleared away for the good of a student.

Miller recognizes that there will be advances in knowledge and the organization of knowledge, and a liberal education will invite these. The curriculum and how it is taught should not remain fixed. The issue is the "undue optimism" or the lack of intellectual humility that would look to find a shortcut to liberal education. As someone who works in teacher education, I don't want to be seen as disparaging the development of better ways of teaching or advocating a position where professors don't see a need to improve their pedagogy. The problem, as I see it, is how the vulnerabilities of the struggling teacher are often preyed upon by the ever-growing education industry, where tips and tricks are sold and sought. When the teacher realizes that these tricks don't work, they (and their students) have lost another year (while the person selling them is long gone). Miller—and, like him, William James in his wonderful talks to teachers[115]—wants us to be on guard against quick fixes so that we might build a foundation for a career of growth as a teacher. Instead of jumping to embrace the next thing, it is often more important to discover our own presence in the classroom and then think about the ways we can use our presence to connect students to each other and the curriculum. Certain teaching techniques (I, for example, resonate with visible thinking[116]) will be useful, but the key element is knowing who we are, knowing what we hope to accomplish and only then thinking about teaching methods, tools, and techniques.

At the risk of digging into the nitty gritty of teaching at the college level, I worry that we are a bit beholden to the myth of the natural-born teacher and don't do enough to help new professors develop a foundation that will lead to sustained excellence in the classroom.[117] By the myth of the natural-born teacher, I mean the belief that a professor either has it or they don't. If they do, they are good candidates for tenure. If not, they get cast into pedagogy workshops and hope for the best. By contrast, it is worth remembering that good teachers should get better and that struggling teachers can also improve. To improve teaching, the first step might not be training in pedagogy, it can be giving teachers a chance to reflect on their own strengths and weaknesses in the classroom and out. After this critical self-reflection, time should be set aside for them to think about the goals of teaching as they relate to liberal education. Only then can they think about how to draw on their own strengths while improving areas of weakness so that they can lead students to meaningful and ambitious goals. Finding a new technique for annotating a text or leading a discussion is useful, but it should be part of a more holistic approach to making progress as a teacher. Undue optimism can keep us from pursuing this broader approach to developing good teaching.

If schools and colleges focused on this holistic approach, they would be less likely to pursue fads, and they would also realize the centrality of presence and character in teaching. As we probably know from experience, two teachers using nearly identical techniques or technologies can get very different responses from a group of students. (We may have found this out the hard way; for example, by bringing back a technique from a conference or a workshop that worked for another teacher and finding it doesn't work for us.) One teacher may get a great discussion started after using clickers or other forms of technology, while another may get an effective discussion started by allowing students long wait time and silent reflection. In teaching, especially liberal education, we must not neglect the significance of the person doing the teaching.[118] Though some methods, technologies, or techniques may be found effective across various contexts and work for different types of teachers, this shouldn't lead us to believe that we will eventually find the one best thing.[119] A technique is enacted and embodied through the person of the teacher. This realization becomes central to Miller's thinking on effective administration of liberal education.

§

I appreciate how blunt Miller is: "No one engaged in liberal teaching should expect all practical arrangements to suit his taste."

What can be read negatively is, as I see it, an appreciation for liberal education. Because we aren't engaged in training, where there is clear output and one efficient way of getting to the output, liberal education will always rely on judgment and compromise. Because there is no one best way to provide students with a liberal education, only pitfalls that should be avoided, we will always remain in touch with our human fallibility. Though this means some arrangements won't be to our taste, or to our taste all of the time, it will mean that we remain free. Unlike other human acts that approximate mechanization and operate under efficiency paradigms, liberal education is free, because its laws are always being discovered by men and women taking responsibility for their discovery.

To make this statement less declarative and more concrete, it might help to remember those fateful moments in our own education. What book, conversation, performance, or experiment gave us an intimation of our nascent powers and the confidence to freely pursue them? After thinking about this, we can wonder why it is that some books or conversations or performances or experiments ignite one student's passion and leave another cold. And here we can puzzle over one of the major difficulties of administrating a liberal education. Our goal should be to give every student as many experiences as possible with those fateful experiences of freedom, remembering that a fateful experience for one student may feel meaningless to another. Because there is no guaranteed path to success, we must rely on judgment, and this means that some of the things we do will fail some of the time for some of our students. The hope is that we will succeed more often than we fail, and that every student will leave with at least some fateful experiences with their freedom.

It takes a person of character to willingly take responsibility for a process that is both so important and so uncertain. Someone who glibly assumes that they can finally figure out the best educational arrangement is really unfit for the role, just as someone who fears the inevitability of some degree of failure and some upset constituents will be unwilling to take on the role. As Miller writes: "Practical arrangements will inevitably reflect the view of personal living which administrators entertain and embody. When the offering of courses, the balance of departments or the scheduling of classes is the care of [people] whose own outlook and personal habits are reflective, modest, and humane, one can trust the result." Here are lines that should be in search committee materials for administration jobs and in documents related to chairing a department or academic committee. Given the inevitability of conflict and the necessity of compromise, the person in the role of college leader will need to be "reflective, modest and humane." The person and their policies stand in something like a symbiotic relationship. A wise person with good judgment chooses sound policy, and sound policies lead to opportunities to be more reflective, more modest, and more humane. It becomes a virtuous cycle. By contrast, small-minded policies that are not aligned with the mission of liberal education often provoke resistance, and the leader responsible for these narrowing policies will often double down on the policy. This keeps them from learning what it would mean to act reflectively, modestly, and humanely.

Miller is drawing our attention to some things that "neoliberal" managers cannot accept: the reality that people are not interchangeable and that perfect solutions to the dynamic and free practice of education are impossible; furthermore, they shouldn't be put forward as ideals and most certainly should not guide decision making. When looking for a leader or when taking on the responsibilities of leadership, we have to appreciate the significance of an individual's character. The final sentence of this section is one very much worth remembering: "If education produces character, it should never be forgotten that it also proceeds from character." Dwelling with this line, we are called to take seriously the charge of a liberal arts college to educate character, and to appreciate that education proceeds from character. At the risk of using antiquated language, we can see the life of a small college as animated by a covenant that each member of the college, especially its administrators and other leaders, must embody and enact.[120] If the mission of a college aims to cultivate broadminded, virtuous, wise, and generous graduates, its students should experience these at the college through as many interactions as possible.[121] To have this experience, everyone at the college should aspire to embody the mission, and holding leaders accountable to the spirit of the covenant should be encouraged. The language of finance and finances will always have its place, but it should not be the only voice. This may seem overly idealistic, but it goes back to trust. If we trust in the power of liberal education, we should trust its wisdom when planning the "offering of courses, the balance of departments . . . the scheduling of classes," and much else. Importantly, this will only create a virtuous cycle. Wise policies create wise decisions and wiser community members, and this in turn allows a community to become wiser.

Returning to points made earlier in this section, when we are working with new professors who are struggling in the classroom, it is important to keep the centrality of character in mind. Our character as mentor to new professors will often do more to determine their success than any explicit teaching technique that we teach or tell them to pursue. If individuals in an academic department are difficult to work with, if they don't exhibit character in their professional work, Miller suggests that the policies in the department won't create the type of freedom that allows good work to flourish. Young faculty who thrive in these departments do so despite the character of the department, not because of it. Just as the myth of the natural-born teacher can get in the way of supporting a life of successful teaching, failure to account for the ways character determines the culture of a college keeps us from appreciating how senior members of faculty can influence the ways that new faculty thrive or struggle. It may seem odd to credit senior members of a department as teacher educators, but they can have a major influence on the type of teaching that new faculty feel empowered to do.[122]

To close, it is good to avoid undue optimism, but it is also important that more senior faculty members see the ways in which their character influences the cultures of teaching and learning that occur in their departments. The best hypothetical defense of liberal education means very little next to what a student experiences of a liberal education in their classes and with their teachers. As such, if we care about liberal education, we will appreciate the ways in which our character will often determine the ways that this education will be experienced, and thus valued, by our students, their parents, and new colleagues coming into our departments.

SECTION 10: COMMUNITY

My discussion of section 9 closed with a brief discussion of a covenant-based community, and section 10 turns squarely to the importance of college as a "vehicle of community." Remember also that section 8 focused on the importance of each individual pursuing a liberal education going their own way, but the outcome of this self-reliant trust is not solipsism or mere individualism. It is hope in the creation of more authentic community. If each of us freely pursues our inquiry, Miller hopes the result will be a community of free inquiry. As he writes in section 10: "For a free country, the concept of community does not consist in agreement on specific truths, but rather on the form of these." Here, a philosopher like John Dewey would draw our attention to the way science works. Scientists don't agree before an experiment what the outcome must be (otherwise it wouldn't be an experiment); they agree on the rules we use to call an experiment authentically scientific. In this way, science is a model for democracy, because it represents a form of community that is in agreement on the *form* of inquiry but not its results.[123] As Dewey understands it, there cannot be a Republican science or a Democrat science; there is only science.

Miller is doing something similar here, though he does not rely on science as a model of inquiry. His paradigm is the process of liberal education. He proposes that liberal "colleges take themselves seriously as the vehicle of community." Drawing again on the idea of a covenant-based community, I see Miller making the claim that a college community can be a form of community that brings freely inquiring individuals together. There are no "specific truths" that individuals at a liberal college must agree to, but they must agree about the "form of these"; they must affirm their belief in free inquiry. Here, an example may help, because it seems impossible, especially in our time, that a community can be created out of nothing more than trust in inquiry itself. One way of thinking about this is to contrast free inquiry with closed inquiry. Closed inquiry sets the outcome that inquiry *must* come to. Here we might think about classrooms where correct thinking is enforced. In these classrooms there may be the appearance of free inquiry, but in these classrooms there are clear rewards and punishments for the results of inquiry.[124] By contrast, an open institution doesn't put guardrails on what can be thought or mandate the necessary outcomes of inquiry, though this doesn't mean that anything is allowed. Though specific truths cannot be mandated in advance of inquiry, liberal colleges remain vigilant about academic standards appropriate to disciplines. For this reason, practices like peer review remain central, and conspiratorial beliefs will be found lacking by the standards of academic disciplines. A recent reboot of the "Sokal affair"[125] has drawn attention to the ways peer review may not be as open or successful as we trust it is, but the very idea that scholars see the importance of policing the quality of peer review signifies its importance in building a truly free community of inquiry.[126]

What Miller helps us think about is the continual risks of free inquiry, especially free inquiry not tied to the relative certainties of agreed-upon methods in the sciences. How can we trust that giving an individual the freedom to think won't result in the revival of flat earth belief and worse? How can we trust that when we free a student from arriving at a guaranteed outcome—be it belief in a religion or political party—it won't lead to disenchantment, incurable skepticism, nihilism, and lack of morale? The problem is that these are all very real risks of liberal education, but they are risks we willingly take on in the name of freedom. Miller writes, "Their authority will be obscure if they see this authority beyond themselves. It must reside in them. They must exemplify in their studies and ceremonies the secular authority of thought." There is no guarantor outside of the college that gives liberal education its authority. This authority must be claimed with each class of students, in each class meeting, in the very ceremonies and policies of the school. It is demanding, but it is a life we freely pursue and advocate as members of a liberal college community. Though the certainties of ideology have their appeal, not least because they guarantee us a community of like-minded believers, and though things like the Sokal hoaxes and conservative attacks can make us lose heart or become cynical, we commit to free inquiry because we hope to create a different form of community. We don't want students to have to accept anything we say simply because we say it; we hope to create a community that shares beliefs because each individual freely comes to that belief on their own.

One thing I value deeply about St. Lawrence University is the tripartite structure of its committees. For each committee, there are faculty representatives, staff representatives, and student representatives. Students are invited into conversations about things like academic policies around plagiarism, not merely to provide input from the student's perspective; it is an opportunity for the student to see that a community is built from the freely given investment of individuals. Most people come into a committee meeting advocating, often very strongly, a position. But we come together in order to determine what is best for the community as a whole, and the process generally works. To put it more positively: it works as well as the human process of free inquiry can. Students quickly learn the importance of holding beliefs strongly while being open to compromise. In this way they learn free inquiry in action.

It is frustrating to think that involving students in committee work can be interpreted as liberal colleges either pandering to students or falling into the "snowflake" trap, reneging on our responsibilities as authorities by letting students determine how they will be educated. Nothing is further from the truth. If we want students to graduate capable of handling the burdens of freedom, then we have to give them opportunities to exercise freedom.[127] One way of doing this is through things like tripartite committee work.

Liberal colleges are under attack, and often because they are seen as too permissive or too ideological. A liberal college necessarily runs these types of risks, but I think a more honest assessment of these colleges will show that they continue to be vehicles of community, often communities that offer a sharp rebuke to the partisan and often mindless bickering on offer by popular news media and our politics. One of the great values of being at a small residential liberal arts college is the sense of responsibility students develop for the college. By acknowledging the desire students have to take responsibility, and by giving them opportunities to exercise responsibility, we are not being permissive—quite the opposite.[128] And by giving students a voice in important conversations that immediately impact them—especially topics that can be controversial in the popular discourse, like gender neutral bathrooms or policies around sexual violence—we are practicing what it means to inquire freely and nonideologically.

As mentioned at the beginning of this book, one of Miller's main goals for liberal education is to teach students the morale that comes when they freely take on the responsibilities of being a trustee for something they value. Small residential liberal arts colleges are spaces that embody this type of trusteeship, housing rare manuscripts and departments of study that may not be popular or economically viable but deeply important nonetheless, and it is also a space where students learn the power of holding something in trust, especially an imperfect thing that doesn't come backed with an ideological guarantee. In this light, the closing lines of section 10 ring especially poignant. Miller writes: "I notice the growing importance of the problem of morale, in the nation and in the schools. And it may be ventured that morale can occur only apropos of something intrinsic, a present value, sportive and severe. If the liberal education is not now the vehicle of morale, what is?"

It is hard to believe that Miller's thinking on liberal education was written seventy-five years ago, because the problem he highlights has, I believe, only gotten worse. Recent analysists looking at the election of Donald Trump point out that many of his most ardent supporters are deeply lonely people.[129] But they are not alone in their loneliness. Though the right often lambasts college students as snowflakes for bravely acknowledging their anxiety, depression, and loneliness, recent surveys show that loneliness is a growing problem for all Americans, a fact made earlier by sociologist Robert Putnam.[130] Miller felt something like this was a problem in 1943, and he suggests that we address morale by freeing students to experience "something intrinsic, a present value, sportive and severe." I will return to this suggestion in a moment. Before doing that, I want to highlight the possibility that liberal education, far from being the threat that its detractors make it out to be, offers a great promise that we should do more to appreciate. As Miller notes, I think very correctly, "If the liberal education is not now the vehicle of morale, what is?"

At the risk of using autobiography as argument, I know that the liberal education I received instilled a deep morale in me. If nothing else, liberal education empowers students to take control of their own education, showing them that there are countless and potentially unending, because always-renewing, conversations to be had about matters centrally important to human life.[131] It may be a very trite way of putting it, but how can someone be alone if always engaged in this type of conversation? While the sociality of Facebook may feel more community-oriented, the solitary act of reading a challengingly meaningful book may do far more to create the type of community that so many Americans seem to be hungering for. Again, at the risk of being cliché, I was most at home when I left the conversations happening around me in high school and entered the world of reading.[132] I don't think this was a retreat that made me unfit for the real world. Rather, it was a fateful act that allowed me to engage the world as my better self. As Miller puts it, liberal education is "something intrinsic, a present value, sportive and severe." Though the world of price is often taken to be "the real world," the world of intrinsic value is equally real, though free. More, it doesn't make one disconnected or joyless: it is sportive and severe. By sportive I hear echoes of Miller's thinking that education is an adventure, and by severe I see parallels with Miller's thinking on "existential learning." Existential learning occurs when we draw out counterbalancing pressures to thinking, holding them in tension to create new possibilities for action. Liberal education prepares us to exercise local control. It empowers us to take up the very real responsibilities as trustees of things we find valuable in our daily lives.

Becoming this type of trustee is both a deeply personal and a public act. It is personal, because we have to do the hard work of discovering what we freely value. At the same time, it is a public act, because we stand up as defenders of what we value through our actions and our very presence in the world. More, by publicly holding what we value, we find community with others who share the same values and who understand the importance of valuing.[133] The liberal arts college is where this type of community is exemplified. Though individuals within departments deeply disagree with each other, and though different departments investigate the world in different ways, at heart they all act as trustees of something valuable. They form a community that is all too rare in the world, and they offer the promise of morale to a culture that seems to be in deep need of it. Free inquiry, inquiry freed from the safety of external guarantees of success and ideological certainty, needn't lead to loneliness and disconnection: it can lead to community and commitment. Liberal education is a kind of solitude that makes a student feel less alone by connecting them with the ongoing conversations of humanity available through their reading and thinking, and it empowers a type of confidence in students that allows them to reengage the world as free individuals capable of the cocreation of more educative forms of community.[134]

SUMMARY: THE ATTRACTION OF COMMITMENT

One of my favorite lines from John Dewey's *Democracy and Education* is "Frontal attacks are even more wasteful in learning than in war."[135] What Dewey is getting at here is the futility of direct argument, especially with students. If we want a student to see a position as worthy of their time and attention, it is far better to exemplify why this is the case than try to argue or shame them into it.

I bring this up here because I worry that liberal education has been under attack for a very long time, and being under attack often leads to the desire to counterattack or the retreat to defensiveness.[136] Though it is only natural to want to defend something we value, it is worth keeping in mind that frontal attacks, even when they are defensive, are often wasteful. This is a point Miller brings to our attention in his summary. Though we want to defend liberal education against detractors, he reminds us that the best defense of liberal education may be to let it stand in its most attractive form. This is something Miller does throughout his notes on liberal education, and he closes these notes by asking us to have faith in the power of liberal education, because liberal education alone is an education fit for a free person willingly taking up the fateful experience of freedom. Someone who is not willing to take on this freedom, who seeks the safe shelter of one form of ideology or another, will only be able to attack and defend, attacking anything out of line with their ideology and defending that ideology when it is called into doubt. Miller asks us not to worry about those types of people, or not to worry about them directly. As Emerson so helpfully remarks in "Self-Reliance": "Do your work, and I shall know you. Do your work, and you shall reinforce yourself."[137] I believe Miller is asking us to do the same thing. Live your defense of the liberal arts, do the work of becoming liberally educated, and you will have your own attraction.

This can be hard advice to take, especially when the future of liberal education is in doubt and its present under attack. But it is worth recalling Miller's thinking in section II: "Nothing is liberal in effect unless it can become a calm possession of a confident mind." This may be one of the hardest lessons to live. Our defense of liberal education must become a calm possession of a confident mind, or else it risks becoming self-defeating.

If we believe in liberal education, then we also believe that an individual must come to appreciate this form of education freely. We cannot "sell it" or shame someone into seeing the good of liberal education or bring someone to appreciate it through fear or coercion. All we can do is continue doing our work, trusting that this will prove attractive enough to remind people of the value of freedom. Continuing to live our defense of liberal education creates a presence that will prove attractive to anyone who hopes to undergo the process of becoming free. This can be small solace, though, when it seems like the louder and less self-possessed voices are garnering the most attention. But Miller urges us to remain confident in the power of liberal education.

The power of liberal education consists "in personal freedom and self-knowledge, and this, in turn, must take the form of a quest for laws. Laws and their exemplars alone possess steady prestige, for they are the loci of both control and growth." Here I am reminded of the power of commitment. Though the liberal educator may not have the immediate power of the ideologue or the dogmatist, they have something else. The loudest voices in the room can convince for a time, might even trump reasonableness for a time, but the only thing that can ever "possess steady prestige" is the lawful exploration of freedom. What we can do for our students, what Miller certainly did for his own students, is to stand as an exemplar of the lawful exploration of freedom, trusting that this is attractive in its own right. We live our defense of liberal education each day, acting as a presence in the lives of students that demonstrates why the adventure of freedom is still worth taking in a world that seems to flatten everything to interchangeability and price. The pursuit of "personal freedom and self-knowledge" is intrinsically valuable and it remains open to us to stand as trustees of the intrinsically valuable, creating a powerful educative presence for our students that offers the promise of freedom from the loneliness and illiberal thinking that so often surrounds them.

§

These reflections on Miller's thinking have covered a lot of ground. Though at points the discussion touched on similar, if not the same, themes, I see this more in line with something like a spiral curriculum than mere repetition.[138] That is, we circle around key ideas, deepening our understanding of terms like morale and presence as we introduce connections between these terms and new topics.[139] As promised at the outset of this book, I turn now from offering commentary on Miller's notes on liberal education and to the practice of teaching at liberal arts colleges.

The next, and final, chapter is meant to be something like a guide to self-reflection on our presence as liberal educators. Given what I've written about how a teacher develops their strengths in the classroom, I won't be offering up methods or techniques that are meant to be implemented. Rather, my aim is to offer questions that help us think about our sense of why liberal education is important and how we can embody its importance in our day-to-day life with students. I believe, with Miller, that this must involve us in the development of "personal freedom and self-knowledge, and this, in turn, must take the form of a quest for laws," in this case the quest for laws that will guide us in developing as effective liberal educators. The questions and ideas in the next chapter are meant to help us do that.

CHAPTER FOUR

CONCLUSION: DEVELOPING PRESENCE

Earlier in this book I make the point that it is often easier for an academic to be critical than it is for them to be appreciative. I find this is often the case when I sit down to write about teaching. Because it is something I value, something I am devoted to, it is very easy to spot poor practice. As my criticism of the edupreneurial industry makes very clear, teaching is not something that can be automated and made easier. It requires devotion and presence, and it is always tied to the person and the character of the educator. This intimate connection between person and professor makes it hard for me to read or offer advice to fellow teachers, or think in general terms about teaching, because the work of teaching is so personal. We can feel this, for example, in those moments where someone accidentally walks into our seminar space, or when a fire drill interrupts a discussion. All of a sudden, we are awakened from this very close communal space and are reminded that the world outside exists. I often think about teaching like this. When it is working, a presence is created, a community comes into existence that is utterly unique to that time and place. As such, it can be difficult to see what someone could teach a professor that would be of value to *that* unique communal experience and the presence of the educator that exists in those moments.

But I also realize the importance of forging a broader community of liberal educators that transcends the closed door of the seminar. There are new and experienced teachers who may not know that feeling of intimacy that can exist between a class and its discussions, and as I criticized the myth of the natural-born teacher earlier in this book, I think it is important to do more to help teachers see their practice as something that can always deepen and improve. Though teaching will always remain a personal art, I hope it isn't an exercise in futility to offer some general suggestions about teaching that aim to connect to who you are, in your classroom, even in those moments when the world outside seems to fade away as you bring student, text, and discussion together, creating a fateful experience of freedom. My suggestions will revolve around three ideas, all drawn from Miller's thinking on liberal education: 1) We teach who we are, 2) we teach in place, and 3) we teach trust and trusteeship. Thinking about these ideas will, I hope, help us establish presence in our classrooms, one that will prove deeply educative for our students while allowing us to continue to grow in our own teaching practice.

In many ways, the question I try to help us think through is: What is keeping you from being present, here-and-now, with your students? How you answer that question may be very different from mine, though there may be important areas of shared concern. The pressure or desire to do research, the need to balance family and personal life with teaching, the feelings of difficulty connecting with young people, the feelings of difficulty keeping your passion alive for your discipline especially as you are asked to do more nonteaching and nonresearch-related work. I imagine we hold some of these concerns in common, though we live them in different ways. What I hope to do in this final chapter is provide resources that empower morale as you find ways to clear away, or manage, those things that stand in the way of being present, of establishing your presence, in your daily work with students and as a representative of liberal education. My guiding principle, one drawn from Miller, is that the work of liberal education opens a space of possibility and an opportunity to experience intrinsic value in a world of price. Remaining in touch with the realm of the intrinsically valuable empowers us to stave off demoralization and remain present with students so that they might grow into trustees of something that they hold to be of value and worth.

§

1) We Teach Who We Are

A key takeaway from Miller's thinking on liberal education is that just as liberal education builds character, the character of the individuals and community doing the educating determines the quality of the education students receive. Though the message is uplifting, it also places a burden of responsibility on the shoulders of liberal educators. It is not enough that we teach our subjects conscientiously and effectively; we must be exemplars of liberal education if we are to educate well.[140] I've had occasion to draw on Miller's appreciation for Emerson several times in this book, and I find that a line from Emerson's "Circles" gets to the heart of the matter when it comes to character and teaching: "Men imagine that they communicate their virtue or vice only by overt actions, and do not see that virtue or vice emit a breath every moment."[141]

I know that if my mind is somewhere else, even if I am saying all of the right things in office hours or during class, I am failing my students, and they can sense this. I may be performing the role of teacher effectively through my overt actions, but overt actions are not all. My presence communicates my character. Initially, as a new teacher, I felt a great deal of pressure in this realization. I felt that I could perfect the external elements—always prepared for class, always returning student work promptly and with copious feedback, always ready to defend my students from whatever got in the way of their education—but I worried a great deal about the "breath" I was emitting in my class, because I worried that this was something I could not control in the way I could control, for example, my instructional planning.

As I've lived as a teacher, I've come to see that my preparation is certainly a key element in my presence. Being a professor who takes preparation seriously establishes a presence of seriousness in the classroom. As well, taking the way you give student feedback seriously communicates a great deal to students about how seriously you take them. If anything, this is one of the most important elements of effective teaching at a liberal arts college. Our class sizes are often very small, we have the freedom to teach subjects that we care about, and we hope to inspire our students to freely consider those subjects and make them their own. If we see feedback as a key element in helping a student develop, we will enter into the work of providing feedback with the seriousness and care it deserves. Instead of sending students the message—either overtly or through the Emersonian breath—that "grading" papers is keeping us from doing more important things, we can use feedback to communicate that we care enough to want students to care about their own work.[142] Our organization, preparation, and feedback forms our character as an educator, and this character is communicated very clearly to students. Though we cannot control what our character communicates in the ways we can control the attention we bring to preparing and giving feedback, this doesn't mean our presence is outside of our control completely.

As well, I often ask my students to reflect on what they look for in good teachers, and they overwhelmingly answer that they look for teachers who are passionate about their subject. When I press them on what they mean by this, they expand their thinking to include things such as: they obviously love what they are teaching; they really want us to understand what they are teaching, and they seem happy when we "get it"; they seem to enjoy being in the classroom with us. What these types of comments circle around is the sense that learning can be joyful. Here is where we have to be mindful of balancing effective planning and the desire to control the learning experience with a willingness to step back in wonder and be appreciative and grateful for the work of teaching. To start, our best plans will be disrupted, a student will routinely say something unexpected, and how we respond to and manage these moments forms our character as educators. If we get overly frustrated by disruption, this will form our presence. If we are able to improvise, turning any moment to an educative purpose, then this also forms our presence. As well, it is easy to forget just how lucky we are to have a hand in the process of education. We often see young people at their best and their worst, and it is important to appreciate that we can positively impact a student's interest in taking responsibility for their education and the direction of their life through the ways we respond to them at their best and worst. It is important that we think a great deal about how we want to respond to a student when they are struggling or when they appear disinterested. Though we may not see it as part of our job as college professors to reach every single student and communicate our passion to them in a way that inspires their own passion for learning, we should recognize that our sense of what our job is will be very clearly communicated to our students and will influence how they learn—or not—in our classroom.

Again, the point here isn't to add to the pressure we feel as professors, but to think about the ways our sense of vocation, as liberal educators, creates a presence that communicates our passion—or lack thereof—to students. How we see our calling as professors will determine how we prepare and give feedback, just as it will inform the ways we improvise in the classroom and how hard we work to make sure that each and every student gets something from our class. Do we send an e-mail to the student who seems distracted by his or her phone, reminding them of the values that they are missing by making this choice, or do we just take off points? Do we take offense when a student seems disengaged, or do we reach out to conference briefly with the student? Do we even notice when a student's engagement seems low and do we do something in response? How we answer these—and countless other questions—will determine our character as teachers and our presence in the classroom.

Finally, engaging with someone like Miller helps us refine our sense of what it means to be liberally educated people. Part of establishing our presence in the classroom is striving to become exemplary of the education we are providing our students. If it is impossible for us to practice the virtues of liberal education, our students see this. For example, if it is impossible for us to dispassionately engage with thinkers or ideas we disagree with, this communicates to students the meaning of liberal education. By contrast, if we are able to patiently empower a student to work through an argument—not interjecting too forcefully, asking the right questions that allow the student to think for themselves—a student comes to experience liberal education in a very different way. I bring this up to stress the importance of continuing to think through the meanings of liberal education, because how we think about liberal education will influence how we teach. An exercise I have my students who plan to teach in secondary schools do is to list one to three non-negotiables. I tell them that teaching, especially at the secondary level, is very fast paced, and a teacher will feel pulled in countless directions. Unless a teacher is mindful of their guiding principles, they can slide into practices that they will, on reflection, not readily assent to. For this reason, it is important that a teacher has a strong sense for the ends of education and that they make sure their practice remains in touch with these in the daily work of teaching.

When the support new professors get is only focused on techniques and activities to do in the classroom, we can easily lose the point of liberal education. For me, a non-negotiable aspect of liberal education is that it should impact a student. Liberal education is not a set of texts or ideas that a student learns, it is something that empowers them to take an interest in their world and take ownership of their power to shape their own thinking. Having this strong sense of purpose in mind helps me select readings, assignments, and assessments, because anything that doesn't help me help a student take responsibility for their thinking—regardless of its other merits—is something that I will drop in favor of something that furthers this purpose. Because I have a strong sense of this non-negotiable, I feel that I can exert what Miller calls "local control." I am making a choice to do some activities and not others, and I willingly live with the consequences. I don't, because I can't, do everything in my classroom, but I am willing to stand behind my decisions, even as I remain open to revising my principles and the activities and texts I use to enact them.

I bring this up not to establish my own virtues as a teacher but to encourage readers to consider their own vision of liberal education so that they can aspire to live that vision, empowering students to become liberally educated in turn. We teach who we are. The more we do to work to become liberally educated the better the results will be for our students. The best defense of liberal education we have is our own example in our classrooms. A student who gets feedback informed by a liberally educated character will have a qualitatively different educational experience than someone who does not. If we believe this, and if we live this faith, we will establish a presence in our classrooms that will sustain our morale and inoculate us against fads and other hindrances to freeing our students to take responsibility for becoming educated. More, if we have a strong vision of the liberally educated person in mind when we plan our courses, we will select more meaningful activities and readings for our students than if this vision is not present to us.

§

2) We Teach in Place

Just as we teach who we are, we teach where we are. To be present in our classrooms, we must feel grounded in our work. In the previous section, I mentioned that if my mind is elsewhere, my students can sense this. To expand on this point, I mean that if I am worried about something going on outside the classroom, this pulls me away from the classroom, keeping me from being present. In this section I am more concerned with something like an existential sense of not being present where we are.[143]

Earlier in the book I mentioned how the job market in higher education can make it hard to establish a presence in place, because there is a sense that there might be a better job out there somewhere. This sense can become a voice that pulls us away from presence: Why work so hard on giving students feedback when you could be doing research that gets you a better job somewhere else? Or, even if we aren't actively looking to leave where we are teaching, the voice of something like a maximizing drive can pull us away from the classroom. By *maximizing drive* I mean the sense that everything in our lives can be made better or more efficient, often through technology. For example, when I travel I find it hard to make simple decisions about where to get coffee or get lunch, because I can read so many reviews about what the best option might be. Because the proliferation of review sites makes it seem like there is a way to "win" lunch or coffee, it feels foolish to settle for something that isn't the best. I think this drive can also pull us away from the classroom. I've heard professors at other colleges lament the quality of their students, and from these comments I see this maximizing thinking at work. Instead of realizing the strength of what is in front of them, the voice that tells them they don't have "the best" pulls them away from being present with the students they do have. Finally, it is hard to establish a presence in place when we are so attuned to the limitations and contingency of every position.[144] That is, every place that has a history is likely to have aspects of that history that are regrettable and worse. More, every place that exists in the world exercises local control: foreclosing the pursuit of some valuable ends while also making compromises that open the institution up to valid criticisms. Instead of accepting the limitations of all local control, some of us try to think from a space where compromise is unnecessary and where one is completely freed from complicity with injustice. Though I think we would all agree that this type of utopia is impossible, it doesn't mean that this kind of utopian thinking doesn't pull us away from being present where we are. Instead of working within the constraints of where we are placed, we seek to inhabit a place where constraints do not exist.

These are just a few examples of the pressures that can pull us away from establishing a presence where we are placed. To be clear, I am not advocating complacency in the face of injustices and inaction in the face of the limitations of institutional history or arrangements. Rather, I sketch out some of the pressures we feel as a means to helping us think about what it would mean to commit to being present in an institution that is both imperfect in its own ways and uniquely able to educate because of its history, traditions, location, mission, and so on. What does it mean to know that there are other colleges—some better, some worse—and there are other students—some better, some worse—and that you are called to teach these particular students at this particular place and at this particular point in time?

One way I think about questions like this is in terms of loyalty.[145] I feel a deep sense of loyalty to my students. At the same time, I know how contingent my connection to these students really is. They could've very easily selected another college to attend, they could've very easily selected another course to take. But once I've had them in class, I feel a connection to these students that makes me obligated to them and loyal to them. I want the best for these students, and I want to clear away hurdles to their success. This doesn't mean I want less for other students; it just means that bonds of loyalty exist between me and my students that are undeniable. While someone can easily play the cynic here—the connection I have to these students really is a contingent thing, and my time would be better served reserving my energy for other pursuits—I see the ability to develop bonds of loyalty even in the face of contingency as a remarkable thing, one that small liberal arts colleges are uniquely positioned to appreciate and build from.

Saying this, the maximizing trends I spell out above seem to spell the death knell of loyalty. How can anyone be loyal to anything when we know that something better might come along? How can we be loyal to anything when we can see its deep imperfections? How can we by loyal to anything when we know how contingent our attachments often are? Miller helps us respond to these questions by giving us the language of local control. Here, a passage I quoted earlier is extremely useful: "We are demoralized today because we proclaim liberty but no actuality as local control and as revelation. Nothing is to be revered."[146] We are demoralized because we've become adept at proclaiming liberty, which frees us to criticize anything and everything, making us feel as if it is foolish not to proclaim this liberty and free ourselves from local attachments. But by doing this, we destroy the possibility of reverence. Just because something is imperfect, or contingent, or limited doesn't mean it isn't to be revered. We can show reverence for our work as professors by helping students become the best version of themselves, not the best version of some ideal student. We show reverence by making the college we are loyal to the strongest version of itself, developing criticisms that make the "actual shine,"[147] not in disparaging the actual in the light of some impossible ideal. Miller's philosophy of education gives us permission to be fully present with students in the actual world of our imperfect classrooms. This may be his greatest gift to us as professors, especially as the possibility of inhabiting the no-place of unlimited criticism has been made easier given the rise of technology. Miller calls us back to our classroom, so that we might experience the real joys and frustrations of helping a young person learn how to think so that they can develop the morale and self-confidence it takes to keep thinking. He makes loyalty possible, and he frees us to experience the morale of being loyal to where we are placed.

Miller reminds us that we are trustees of this valuable form of education and urges us to not give up on liberal education, even as it remains under relentless attack. Though there are reasons to be critical of liberal education, we can be critical and loyal. One can be a nondogmatic steward or trustee: criticism should not make trusteeship impossible, just as trusteeship should not make criticism impossible. We teach where we are. Though being placed like this brings constraints, they are the types of constraints that establish our presence and give us morale. Our students realize that we are loyal to them, and we realize all of the things we can do in the here-and-now to make their education better. We don't need to publish academic articles or defend liberal education against pundits looking to profit on negativity in order to be a trustee of liberal education. We can redesign our courses so that students are given the opportunity to experience the power of liberal education. We can take our committee work seriously, working to improve the administration of liberal education on our campus. Most important, we can take heart and morale in the realization that we are trustees of real values, and that being this type of trustee forms our character and educates our students.

To close, I think it is important to self-reflect on where we are placed. What keeps us from establishing a presence on our college campuses? Some constraints are insurmountable, and in these cases it is worth absenting ourselves while we look for better places to teach, work, and live.[148] But in other cases, the issue may be more about our mindset. I hope this book helps us think about the ways in which we can ground ourselves in imperfect places, and how this commitment also creates possibilities for loyalty and trusteeship that are valuable. In a world of price, everything is interchangeable. By contrast, in a world of value, we form loyalties. Though one classroom may seem like any other classroom to a consultant, if a classroom is a seminar room where you first started teaching, or where you always teach your first-year seminar, it becomes charged with value. A life of teaching in community with other devoted liberal educators can transform mere classrooms into places of learning, places where students return not only for reunion, but when they are facing conflicts in their life and need to draw on morale to get through. What we do in our classrooms has the power to change the trajectory of a student's life, and we enhance this power significantly when we commit to being fully present where we are.

§

3) We Teach Trust and Trusteeship

In the previous section I mentioned that we teach in place and in time. Our time, especially after November 8th, 2016, is one marked by fear and bitter partisanship. It is hard to be present in the classroom when we feel that our democratic institutions are under attack.[149] More, it can be harder than normal to commit fully to disinterested study if doing this would mean not doing enough to resist what some scholars are heralding as the beginning of American fascism.[150] It can be difficult to be present to every student, if the landscape we are living in encourages an us and them mentality, because this can make it feel as if students with different politics are a threat, and the job of education is to bring students to one side of the political spectrum.

I don't want to downplay the threats of our present moment, but I do wonder if we can find a way to balance the need for political vigilance—whichever political party we belong to—with the need to carve out a space where students can learn how to think and experience a world of value that may only indirectly intersect with the world of politics. Miller contended with similar questions at the end of his life, when college campuses were the sites of serious political protest and when American institutions experienced great shocks: the assassination of a president, civil rights leaders murdered, domestic terrorism, the threat of nuclear annihilation, Vietnam, a president resigning in disgrace. I don't know if much is gained by exploring whether the threat to American institutions is greater now than it was then, but comparing our present difficulties to what America survived in the past makes me hopeful that a commitment to liberal education in our time is not tantamount to Nero's fiddling. Miller's stance, especially his perception of student protest as a potential threat to liberal education, is one that may be especially unpopular, politically, now.[151]

Miller's stance may be particularly unpopular for at least two reasons. First, and like civil rights lawyer Pauli Murray, an African American woman responsible for developing arguments that led to the *Brown v. Board* decision, Miller felt that liberal colleges were run by the best judgments of the faculty: they shouldn't be in the business of accepting demands from students.[152] This is a position that may seem too elitist and too unresponsive to the concerns of students who feel disempowered and voiceless. On the other hand, the same faculty members who may invite the populist energies of student protest may be particularly aversive to the types of populism that brought Donald Trump to power.[153] What Miller causes us to think about, as trustees of institutions of liberal education, is how responsive we should be to explicitly political demands, especially when these demands can undermine educational values. Though we must discuss the ways in which the works assigned at liberal arts colleges are exclusionary or disempowering or not inclusive enough, we shouldn't bend to student demands that certain works are either automatically assigned or automatically excluded.[154] A student is not in a position to be a trustee for liberal education. Asserting this is not to wield our authority as trustees in an authoritarian fashion or to silence student questions or concerns.[155] Liberal education is about asking difficult questions, and allowing students the power to censor authors and texts they've never read is irresponsible. Inviting students into conversations about why texts are selected and continue to be assigned is important, especially if they are going to develop into future stewards of liberal education. Giving them premature power keeps this from happening, just as failing to teach them about how curricular decisions are responsibly made does.

The second, and related, reason why Miller's politics might

be unpopular to some liberal educators is that they are complicated by the fact that they are motivated by a deeply conservative impulse and an impulse driven by the democratic belief that we must each take responsibility for our thinking. This puts him in an unfashionable middle ground. For Miller, liberal education is fundamentally about conserving something: namely, the possibilities of liberal education. Liberal colleges, to preserve the possibilities of liberal education, may need to seek freedom from immediate relevance, especially the immediate relevance of politics. A student cannot begin thinking liberally about politics if they've never had the experience of thinking liberally. Importantly, though liberal education is removed from practical, especially political, concerns, this does not mean it is placed in an elite and closed-off realm. Quite the opposite. Liberal education is democratic, because it is ultimately open to anyone, so long as they are willing to accept burdens of thinking. Here is where Miller's thinking moves from conserving to something else. We conserve a space where thinking can happen, but once we free someone to think, we cannot predict—and we most certainly shouldn't determine—where this thinking will take them. Here is where we can see liberal education resulting in new politics. The key point, for Miller, is giving a student the experience of liberal thinking before forcing them into the political world. In our fast-paced world, a world of social media that makes it feel that we must pass judgment on every passing news item (or presidential tweet), it can feel self-indulgent or worse to step back, giving our students the gift of four years of relative seclusion from immediate political engagement, letting them grow in power before they reengage with the world.[156]

Complete seclusion, of course, is impossible. But one troubling result of President Trump's election is that although traditional newspapers are experiencing a resurgence of subscriptions, readers of fiction and poetry are dwindling. It only makes sense that someone who is concerned about the direction the country is taking will read more journalism and seek political engagement. But there is also a case to be made for not being completely thrown out of our orbit, for cultivating virtues that aren't immediately political. This is a hard case to make to someone who is convinced that we are steps away from fascism, but it is worth wondering what virtues will be called upon if democracy comes under serious attack. In addition to political virtues, I think of the strength that we can draw on by reading fiction and religious literatures. We can read memoirs of men and women subjected to the terrors of Nazism and see that what empowered their persistence was often lines of poetry or an exemplary figure drawn from history. Liberal educators harbor untold sources of wealth that can be drawn on in times of great stress; focusing narrowly on politics may undercut some of the good that liberal education can do in tumultuous times.[157]

The point I am getting at is that being a trustee of a nonpolitical value is not something to be abandoned, even when it feels as if everyone is called to politics. Keeping the doors open to liberal education is important. Maintaining one's scholarship, even if it feels irrelevant, is important. Being a trustee of liberal education, conserving the spaces that allow liberal education to happen, matters a great deal, even—or maybe especially—in times of political turmoil.

But even in times that are not politically tumultuous, it is good to appreciate the importance of serving as trustees of liberal education. Here, it is useful to draw the distinction between being a guardian or a gatekeeper and serving as a trustee whose aim is to introduce liberal education to as wide an audience as possible. As mentioned earlier, there seems to be a crisis of loneliness in America, and social media only seems to be exacerbating this problem. Liberal education is attractive because it offers an invitation to come out of loneliness and into community with the living and the dead who have devoted their lives to meaningful work. It is an aspirational community, where we are always trying to engage in conversation that deepens our understanding and appreciation of values. I mention that it is different from a gatekeeper model, because I see liberal education as something that anyone can grow into. As a teacher, this is communicated in the feedback I give and in the way I try to make each class a bridge from the student—wherever they are—and into the start of a meaningful conversation. Instead of holding the goods of liberal education out as something that are only experienced near the end of the educational journey, I try to make the first step as attractive as possible.

Here, again, it is worth highlighting how detrimental the snowflake discourse can be. In my experience, students don't want to be sheltered from difficult ideas, but I do feel as if they've internalized a lot of pressure and are worried about failing in college. I've had many students express concern that they wouldn't be able to stay at college because one or both of their parents have been laid off from their jobs, and they want to make sure that everything they do in college ensures that they are successful—not out of a sense of selfishness or entitlement but out of respect for their parents and the sacrifices they are making to send them to college. If we want a student in this position to take the risks of becoming liberally educated, I feel it is worth being very mindful of the types of support they might need in order to take these risks. Most important is showing students that although liberal education is often very difficult, it is something that they can do. We don't have to be patronizing to do this, and we don't have to simplify the curriculum. The goal is to find the right text or activity that serves as the bridge from a student to their liberal education.

When we do this, we free students from loneliness and fear and put them in touch with a conversation that they can always return to and continue to grow in. In a way, this line of thinking brings together political concern and the concern with loneliness in America. Liberal education gives young people an opportunity to join a community that is not premised on acceptance of a creed but is open to anyone with a commitment to thinking. Liberal education, when seen this way, becomes a firewall against authoritarianism and apathy. When we take on the responsibility of liberal education, we think for ourselves and we become a trustee of our values. The promises of demagogues ring hollow, and the cynicism of the lonely is unappealing because the liberally educated person is caring for things they value and are joined in community with other valuers. Again, it isn't a dogmatic community—a community where beliefs are enforced—it is a community of men and women devoted to what they value, inviting others to experience that value and determine its worth in their own lives.

As a liberal educator, it is important that we continue to hold out the invitation to what we value, standing as exemplars of what it means to be a trustee of value in the world. Our students are not snowflakes, though we should remain mindful of the ways that we can sustain their morale through difficult times. Our loyalty to our students, our attempt to be fully present with them, and the example of our trusteeship can give them the confidence it takes to undergo a liberal education. Our presence educates. It is important that we trust this, and that we find ways to grow in this trust. At every level of a liberal arts college, we should remind ourselves that a liberal education starts from the character of the community of liberal educators, and that liberal education is a great good. Though it doesn't respond directly to political or economic pressures, it has a power that emerges when we trust it. The reverse is also true. If we are unwilling to stand as trustees of liberal education, we shouldn't be surprised if it loses its power and appeal. As professors at liberal arts colleges, I hope this book—in some very small ways—helps you connect with the good of liberal education and encourages you to live this good in your daily work. The best argument for liberal education is the character of its representatives, and—for better and worse—this is what we must rely on as we make the attempt to offer up a lived defense of liberal education.

§

To close, liberal education matters. I am grateful that I am in a position to serve as a representative and trustee of liberal education. My Middlebury education transformed me, drawing me from loneliness to community, and I continue to grow in my respect and awe that liberal education exists. Miller used the words reverence and piety in his thinking about liberal education, and they are apt.[158] It remains a wonder that these places exist and that they continue to exert the attraction they do. All is not well, we know this, but being in crisis mode can keep us from trusting in what will always remain valuable about liberal education. It frees students from loneliness and frees them to think. They enter into a community of the liberally educated, a community that is not united in belief, but is a force for good in the world.

I know I didn't promise tips and tricks in this final section, but I do worry that some readers will expect more in terms of things they can do, tomorrow, in their respective classrooms. To this I can only say that trusting in the good that liberal education did for you, or that you've seen it do for your students, will impact the presence you have in the classroom, and that trusting the good of liberal education will allow you to challenge practices and policies that stand in the way of liberal education while also empowering you to exercise the types of pedagogical creativity that build bridges from where your students are to the wonders they might experience if they trust in their own education.

There may not be anything more we can do than this, but it is not nothing. The "calm possession of a confident mind" may seem a small thing in comparison to the loud voices of the pundit, but it has its own attraction. Miller didn't seek the ideal, he didn't seek beyond his small college community, but he created a vision of teaching that is inspiring in its way, reminding us that if we devote ourselves to being a presence for students, we will free them to continue the work of preserving a realm of real value.

Preserving this realm of value, we can hope that our students will also find ways to make our world better in the ways they live as liberally educated women and men. The example of our students, in how they live their liberal education, is the best defense of liberal education we have. Centering our pedagogy around empowering liberally educated graduates who are trustees of value should be a first priority in our classrooms and institutions of liberal education. Doing this will re-moralize us as we balance the self-criticism and commitment necessary to living as an educative presence in the lives of our students.

Notes

1. For a beautiful discussion of aspiration and its role in education, see Agnes Callard, "Liberal Education and The Possibility of Valuational Progress," *Social Philosophy and Policy* 34, no. 2 (2017): 1–22. Her book *Aspiration* (New York: Oxford University Press, 2018) offers similarly rewarding reading.
2. For example, many well-intentioned defenses of liberal education highlight the earning potential of graduates of liberal arts colleges and the numbers of CEOs with liberal arts degrees.
3. For an excellent example of a defense of liberal education that sticks closely to the lived experience of that education, see Talbot Brewer, "What Good Are the Humanities?" *Raritan* 37, no. 4 (2018): 98–118.
4. The John William Miller Fellowship website has an excellent biography and collection of work by and about Miller. See https://sites.williams.edu/miller/.
5. A great starting point for someone interested in Miller is the anthology *The Task of Criticism* (New York: Norton, 2005).
6. Though there are several studies of Miller's work, I find the following two the strongest and very interesting reads in their own right: Vincent Colapietro, *The Fateful Shapes of Human Freedom: John William Miller and the Crises of Modernity* (Nashville, TN: Vanderbilt University Press, 2003) and Michael McGandy, *The Active Life* (Albany: State University of New York Press, 2005). I suggest starting with these titles as they both, albeit in different ways, offer an excellent overview of Miller's philosophy and its significance.
7. McGandy makes the point in *The Active Life*: "In the case of Williams College, Miller was not captivated by a philosophical figure or school. He was transformed and redefined by teaching" (ix). I agree, and this book attempts to demonstrate what it means to be transformed and redefined by teaching.

8. As such, I won't try to be exhaustive in my references. I will use references as invitations to further reading, not as a way of covering ground.
9. Defenses of the liberal arts are legion as are books that aim to give practical guidance to teachers and professors. As I hope to show in this book, Miller's thinking on the liberal arts offers a great, and unique, contribution to these literatures. For other examples of a lived defense, see Brewer, "What Good," and Mark Edmundson, *Why Teach?* (New York: Bloomsbury, 2013).
10. Miller, *The Task of Criticism*, 321.
11. This may be an unhelpful tangent, but when I try to contextualize this talk historically, I am struck by the timing. If anything, the early 1950s can be pointed to as a time when colleges were doing extremely well. (For a discussion of this point, in an admirably interesting essay about liberal education, see Robert Pippin, "Liberation and the Liberal Arts," University of Chicago, website, esp. 5 ff. Retrieved from: https://aims.uchicago.edu/sites/aims.uchicago.edu/files/uploads/pdf/2000-Aims%20Address-Robert%20Pippin.pdf. See, also, Ernest Boyer, *Campus Life: In Search of Community* (Princeton, NJ: Carnegie Foundation for the Advancement of Teaching, 1990), xi). Large numbers of students could attend college because of a growing economy and the GI Bill, and prospects for jobs after graduation and jobs in higher education for PhDs were strong. The unrest brought to college campuses by the Vietnam War and civil rights era were still on the horizon. Why, then, would Miller worry about the morale of college students?
12. "The American Scholar," in Ralph Waldo Emerson, *Essays and Lectures* (New York: Library of America, 1983).
13. Emerson is a touchstone in Miller's published and unpublished works. Though the connection to Emerson is not a major focus in the extant literature on Miller, I think the Emerson–Miller connection is especially strong around education and teaching, so it makes sense that it would come out more strongly in this case than in the existing studies. More, we can see from the very title of this Hobart address that Emerson was on Miller's mind when he thought about education.
14. William Ernest Hocking, "The Nature of Morale," *American Journal of Sociology* 47, no. 3 (1941): 302–20. Though Hocking, like Miller, is not in vogue philosophically, a recently published book on Hocking may change that; see: John Kaag, *American Philosophy: A Love Story* (New York: Farrar, Straus, and Giroux, 2016).
15. Hocking also notes that the morale of America going into the first world war was similarly superficial. We didn't really know what we were getting into, but we were energized to enter the war. In a way, this seems like a bit

of self-criticism, as Hocking wrote a pamphlet on morale to be used by the military in the first war. See: William Hocking, *Morale and Its Enemies* (New Haven, CT: Yale University Press, 1918). As America confronted the reality of a second world war, the question of morale once again arose (see Goodwin Watson, *Civilian Morale* [Boston, MA: Houghton Mifflin, 1942] for an anthology on this issue). Hocking was once again responding to the need for morale in a time of war but placed far more attention on the *quality* of morale and its philosophical implications than some writers who just wanted Americans to have the morale necessary to sustain the war effort.

16. Hocking, "The Nature of Morale," 304.
17. This balance is explored beautifully in Vincent Colapietro's *The Fateful Shapes*.
18. For an excellent discussion of this issue, see Kieran Setiya, "Does Moral Theory Corrupt Youth?" *Philosophical Topics* 38, no. 1 (2010): 205–22.
19. For an excellent discussion of this point, see Marilynne Robinson, "Waiting to be Remembered," *Amherst Magazine*, 2007. Retrieved from: https://www.amherst.edu/amherst-story/magazine/issues/2007_summer/remembered.
20. For an excellent, recent discussion of how liberal arts colleges can and should cultivate student well-being, see: Donald Harward, *Well-Being and Higher Education* (Washington, DC: Association of American Colleges & Universities, 2016).
21. Found in the Miller Papers, housed at Williams College, box 27, folder 27.
22. It is thus slightly ironic that college buildings (and an entire college) are named after Emerson.
23. For an insightful discussion of this type of care, see Milton Mayeroff, *On Caring* (New York: HarperCollins, 1971).
24. Nowhere is this belief clearer than in "The American Scholar," where Emerson writes, "I ask not for the great, the remote, the romantic; what is doing in Italy or Arabia; what is Greek art, or Provencal minstrelsy; I embrace the common, I explore and sit at the feet of the familiar, the low. Give me insight into to-day, and you may have the antique and future worlds" (Emerson, *Essays*, 68–69).
25. For an excellent criticism of this type of optimism, see Stuart Hampshire, *Justice Is Conflict* (Princeton, NJ: Princeton University Press, 2000).
26. For an excellent discussion of teacher as custodian, see James Banner and Harold Cannon, *The Elements of Teaching* (New Haven, CT: Yale University Press, 2017). *The Elements of Teaching* is a beautiful book on teaching that touches on many central themes of this book. As well, I appreciate Samuel Scheffler's argument for the importance of standing in a custodial chain in the wonderful essay "The Normativity of Tradition" found in his *Equality and Tradition* (New York: Oxford University Press, 2012).

27. Miller, *The Task of Criticism*, 317.
28. For an early, but still important, discussion of this, see Hubert Dreyfus, "Anonymity versus Commitment: The Dangers of Education on the Internet," *Educational Philosophy and Theory* 34, no. 4 (2002): 369–78.
29. Miller, *The Task of Criticism*, 321.
30. For an interesting discussion of this point, see Annette Baier, *Reflections on How We Live* (New York: Oxford University Press, 2010), esp. chapters 1 and 2. See, also, Samuel Scheffler, *Why Worry About Future Generations?* (New York: Oxford University Press, 2018).
31. For a reflection on some of these issues, see Jeff Frank, "Resisting Locker Room Talk," *Groundworks* (Philosophy of Education Society, Committee on Professional Affairs, 2019). Retrieved from https://docs.wixstatic.com/ugd/c8f5fb_1561e7e65c444787805954559f9aefe1.pdf
32. When I read Dorothy Allison's beautiful Tanner Lecture, I was glad to see that I was not alone in this feeling (found at https://tannerlectures.utah.edu/_documents/a-to-z/a/Allison_02.pdf, see esp. 321 ff.). Ted Cohen's story "Ethics Class" offers dark humor on doing ethics divorced from feeling. See his *Serious Larks* (Chicago: University of Chicago Press, 2018).
33. For an excellent discussion of the ways the Socratic method has been distorted, see Avi Mintz, "From Grade School to Law School: Socrates' Legacy in Education," in *A Companion to Socrates* (Malden, MA: Blackwell, 2009).
34. I've found that having students read Meira Levinson and Jacob Fay's *Dilemmas in Educational Ethics* (Cambridge, MA: Harvard Education Press, 2016) is one way to help them appreciate how beliefs inform policy and practice in education.
35. In relation to this point, I especially appreciate Judith Shklar's discussion of her own teaching. She writes: "The reason why I teach political theory is not that I just like the company of young people, but that I love the subject unconditionally and am wholly convinced of its importance and want others to recognize it as such. It has therefore been quite easy for me to avoid becoming a guru or substitute parent. I really only want to be a mother to our three children, and do not like disciples. And I fear that the students who so readily attach themselves to idols lose their education along with their independence." Retrieved from https://publications.acls.org/OP/Haskins_1989_JudithNShklar.pdf.
36. For an excellent discussion of this point, see David Hansen, *Exploring the Moral Heart of Teaching* (New York: Teachers College Press, 2001).
37. Cristina Cammarano, "Philosophical Considerations on Teacher Presence," *Philosophy of Education Yearbook 2015*. Retrieved from https://

educationjournal.web.illinois.edu/archive/index.php/pes/article/view/4524.pdf. For another insightful discussion of presence in teaching, see Carol Rogers and Miriam Raider-Roth, "Presence in Teaching," *Teachers and Teaching* 12, no. 3 (2006): 265–87.

38. John William Miller, *In Defense of the Psychological* (New York: Norton, 1983), 87.
39. For a good discussion of being present in the classroom, see Jerry Farber, "Teaching and Presence," *Pedagogy* 8, no. 2 (2008): 215–25.
40. Cammarano, "Philosophical Considerations," 429.
41. Found in the Miller Papers, housed at Williams College, box 22, folder 14.
42. I borrow this language of appreciative understanding from Philip Jackson, an outstanding philosopher of teaching and a teacher to my mentor in graduate school, David Hansen. See Philip Jackson, "John Dewey's 1906 Definition of Art," *Teachers College Record* 104, no. 2 (2002): 167–77.
43. For a discussion of this non-heroic heroism, see Jeff Frank, "Love and Work," *Ethics and Education* 12, no. 2 (2017): 233–42.
44. I return to the idea of reverence in the final chapter.
45. John William Miller, *The Midworld* (New York: Norton, 1982), 191–92.
46. Emerson, *Essays*, 491.
47. Emerson, 492.
48. Miller, *The Task of Criticism*, 314.
49. Cushing Strout, "Truth Is in the Telling," *Bucknell Review* 34, no. 1 (1990), 155.
50. Kwame Appiah, *Cosmopolitanism* (New York: Norton, 2007) and David Hansen, *The Teacher and the World* (New York: Routledge, 2011).
51. Stanley Bates, "Book Notes," *Ethics* 92, no. 1 (1981): 181–82.
52. Though I cannot explore the connection further here, I see a similarity between Miller's position on accepting that one is placed as a means to developing integrity and the position developed by Raimond Gaita in "Moral Understanding" found is his *Good and Evil: An Absolute Conception* (New York: St. Martin's Press, 1991).
53. For a brief discussion of this point, see Jeff Frank, "Technology, Stupor, and the Future of Liberal Arts Colleges," *Hechinger Report*, May 22, 2018. Retrieved from https://hechingerreport.org/opinion-technology-stupefaction-and-the-future-of-liberal-arts-colleges/. See, also, Dini Metro-Roland and Paul Farber, "Lost Causes: Online Instruction and the Integrity of Presence," *Philosophy of Education Yearbook 2010*. Retrieved from: https://educationjournal.web.illinois.edu/archive/index.php/pes/article/view/3031.pdf.
54. Here I am thinking of William Cronon's popular defense of liberal education in "Only Connect," *The American Scholar* 67, no. 4 (1998): 73–80.

55. This is Miller's note. He is very likely referring to Ellwood Patterson Cubberley, *Readings in the History of Education* (New York: Houghton Mifflin, 1920).
56. For one of the most complex and interesting defenses of the great books, see the work of Eva Brann. Brann's position is far more complex than the caricature of the worshipper of books that Emerson critiques, but it does offer a picture of commitment different from Miller's and Emerson's. For a starting point, see her "The American College as the Place for Liberal Learning," *Daedalus* 128, no. 1 (1999): 151–71.
57. For example, Jeffrey Nesteruk writes very insightfully about the connections between liberal education and business education. For an example, see "Business Teaching, Liberal Learning, and the Moral Transformation of Business Education," *Organization Management Journal* 9, no. 2 (2012): 114–19.
58. For a thoughtful defense of teacher education programs at liberal arts colleges, see Eva Travers, "The Case for Teacher Education at Selective Liberal Arts Colleges," *Phi Delta Kappan* 62, no. 2 (1980): 127–31.
59. For a beautiful discussion of this point, see Raimond Gaita, "Goodness and Truth," *Philosophy* 67 (1992): 507–21.
60. Emerson, *Essays*, 57.
61. Here I especially appreciate Michael Roth's *Beyond the University* (New Haven: Yale University Press, 2015) because it draws on American philosophy and philosophers to develop an approach to liberal education in America.
62. Roth, *Beyond*.
63. Here it is interesting to note Alfred North Whitehead's defense of business education in *The Aims of Education* (New York: Free Press, 1929), especially chapter 8. I think Whitehead's way of understanding the multiple purposes of a university education frees us to see how something like business can be taught liberally.
64. It would take an entire book to discuss the status of teacher education at liberal arts colleges. Though I believe teaching can—and should—be taught liberally, the bureaucratic requirements teacher education programs are put under, and the types of assessments that someone must pass in order to become a certified teacher, make it hard to see how teacher education programs can exist at liberal arts colleges. The irony here is that we are making it easier in some ways for people to become a teacher—fast-tracks and alternative routes—and yet deeply constraining what small liberal arts colleges can do. Again, this is a topic for another book, but it strikes me as important for people who would defend teacher education at liberal arts colleges to address how the aims of liberal education can coexist with certification requirements that seem antithetical to the mission of liberal education.

65. For an excellent discussion of the person in teaching, see David Hansen, "Bearing Witness to the Fusion of Person and Role in Teaching," *The Journal of Aesthetic Education* 52, no. 4 (2018): 21–48.
66. There is a strong tradition of helping students think through the moral dimensions of business. For two examples, see Joseph Badaracco, *Managing in the Gray* (Cambridge, MA: Harvard Business Review Press, 2016) and Patricia Werhane, *Moral Imagination and Management Decision-Making* (New York: Oxford University Press, 1999).
67. I can't tell you how frustrating it is when textbook salespeople tell me that they can offer me a package that includes all my lectures and assessments. This is not liberal education.
68. I choose Emerson's language of self-reliance, but one can see parallels between my concerns here and concerns, emanating from Kant's work on education, about how education for autonomy is possible. For an excellent, recent discussion, see Kyla Ebels-Duggan, "Educating for Autonomy: An Old-Fashioned View," *Social Philosophy and Policy* 31, no. 1 (2013): 141–61.
69. The literature on Kant is extensive and very interesting. I offer a thumbnail sketch of Kant's thinking here. Most of my conversation will revolve around his *Groundwork of the Metaphysics of Morals* (New York: Cambridge University Press, 2012). For a discussion of Kant's influence on Miller, which I don't pursue here in detail, see Stephen Tyman, *Descrying the Ideal* (Carbondale, IL: Southern Illinois Press, 1993).
70. For an excellent discussion of Kant's influence on Emerson and the ways Emerson tropes Kant to the American context, see Stanley Cavell, *Emerson's Transcendental Etudes* (Palo Alto, CA: Stanford University Press, 2003).
71. Here I must sidestep debates about how Kant feels about animals and humans with cognitive impairments. I feel Elizabeth Anderson addresses these problems squarely while also holding on to Kant's important insights on value. See her *Value in Ethics and Economics* (Cambridge, MA: Harvard University Press, 1993).
72. For a discussion of this point, see Jeff Frank, "Sheldon Wolin, Jean Vanier, and the Present Age," *Ethics and Education* 13, no. 3 (2018): 360–69.
73. Emerson, *Essays*, 492.
74. I can't pursue this line of thinking here, but there is an important connection between reclaiming "leisure" as a way of speaking back to the way time is commodified. Liberal colleges can do more to help a student value "free" time. For a nice discussion, see Kevin Gary, "Leisure, Freedom, and Liberal Education," *Educational Theory* 56, no. 2 (2006): 121–36.
75. For an inspiring discussion of fear and how we must wrest ourselves from

its grip, see Martha Nussbaum, *The Monarchy of Fear* (New York: Simon & Schuster, 2018).

76. Again, this language may strike some readers as too overzealous. I worry, though, that we are not zealous enough at times. We are outraged by events that are often outside of our control, but the world we inhabit—the life-changing world of the classroom—is ours, and the passion we bring to it remains transformative. For a similar perspective on education and our place in the world, see Marilynne Robinson, *What Are We Doing Here? Essays* (New York: Farrar, Straus, and Giroux, 2018).
77. For an excellent discussion, see Callard, "Liberal Education."
78. I see important and interesting parallels between this argument and Adrienne Rich's argument in "Claiming an Education," found in her *On Lies, Secrets, and Silence* (New York: Norton, 1979).
79. This, as we know, is one of the most gratifying experiences in teaching. A student comes into college thinking they will never find a job and leave with a calling.
80. The sense of power I use here can be confusing. Like the price/value distinction, the power liberal education makes possible is power in the realm of appreciating and cultivating value, though it may not issue forth in power in the normal sense of the word. I use the term "creative power" to gesture toward the sense of power Miller has in mind and that is cultivated by liberal education.
81. Though I've already cited Stanley Cavell's important and influential reading of Emerson, I am often most moved by Richard Poirier's Emerson, because Poirier appreciates how Emerson's work works to unlock the energy of thinking. For more, see his *The Renewal of Literature* (New York: Random House, 1987) and *Poetry and Pragmatism* (Cambridge, MA: Harvard University Press, 1992).
82. I see rich parallels here between Miller's use of adventure and Diamond's use of adventure as applied to the moral possibilities of literature. See her "Missing the Adventure," in her *The Realistic Spirit: Wittgenstein, Philosophy, and the Mind* (Cambridge, MA: MIT Press, 1991) and "Henry James, Moral Philosophers, Moralism," *Henry James Review* 18, no. 3 (1997): 243–57.
83. When teaching first-year students about the liberal arts, I am always surprised by how surprised they are that there are other standards of success than merely material ones. In our current political climate, it seems we are willing to forgive abhorrent moral beliefs if the person holding them is rich or promises to make us rich. For a good guide to discussing this issue with students, see Mark Roche, *Why Choose the Liberal Arts* (South Bend,

IN: University of Notre Dame Press, 2010), Roth, *Beyond the University*, and Martha Nussbaum, *Not for Profit* (Princeton, NJ: Princeton University Press, 2017).

84. Here I am echoing the title of a wonderful book on Leo Tolstoy, Gary Saul Morson's *Hidden in Plain View* (Palo Alto, CA: Stanford University Press, 1987).
85. I feel I would be remiss if I didn't mention Richard Eldridge's excellent work at some point in this book. In addition to writing excellent work on liberal education, Eldridge's book *Images of History* (New York: Oxford University Press, 2016) offers an excellent discussion of how the question of what it means to be a free person will always be a question for us. It is also worth noting that Stanley Bates was Eldridge's mentor when he was a student at Middlebury College.
86. For more on Canada, see his less-known, but excellent, book *Fist Stick Knife Gun* (Boston, MA: Beacon, 2010).
87. See DeRay Mckesson, *On the Other Side of Freedom* (New York: Viking, 2018).
88. One of the best, and earliest, can be found in Sheldon Wolin and John Schaar's *The Berkeley Rebellion and Beyond* (New York: *New York Review Books*, 1970). For contemporary work on the topic, consult Benjamin Ginsberg, *The Fall of the Faculty* (New York: Oxford, 2011). For a classic treatment, see Thorstein Veblen, *The Higher Learning in America* (Baltimore, MD: Johns Hopkins University Press, 2015).
89. For a powerful discussion of this point, see Raimond Gaita, "To Civilize the City," *Meanjin Quarterly* 71, no. 1 (2012). Retrieved from https://meanjin.com.au/essays/to-civilise-the-city/.
90. For a nice, brief treatment, see Jonathan Cole, "Why Sports and Elite Academics Do Not Mix," *Atlantic*, March 19, 2017. Retrieved from https://www.theatlantic.com/education/archive/2017/03/the-case-against-student-athletes/518739/. For a longer treatment in a book that shares many of the perspectives developed in this one, see his *The Great American University* (New York: PublicAffairs, 2009).
91. See his *Freedom and the College* (New York: Century Company, 1923).
92. See his *A Free and Ordered Space* (New York: Norton, 1988).
93. For an interesting discussion of some of these points, see Mark Edmundson, "Does Sports Build Character or Damage It?" *Chronicle of Higher Education* (2012). Retrieved from https://www.chronicle.com/article/Do-Sports-Build-Character-or/130286.
94. Even at highly selective liberal arts colleges, students spend much of the year—in season and out training for their sport. Though there is data that demonstrates students involved in athletics have higher GPAs than their

non-athlete peers, the message of sports can be that academics are instrumental to athletics; an important hurdle, but not really the central focus of a college education.

95. Leon Botstein, *Jefferson's Children* (New York: Doubleday, 1997), 197.
96. Cohen, *Serious Larks*.
97. For an insightful discussion of this point, see Akeel Bilgrami, "Truth, Balance, and Freedom," *Social Research* 76, no. 2 (2009): 417–36. See, also, Michael Berube, *What's Liberal About the Liberal Arts?* (New York: Norton, 2006).
98. This is a controversial topic, but I find myself agreeing with Jeremy Waldron that hate speech is an attack on a person's dignity, and this should give us reason to consider what role hate speech should have in educational institutions where we are concerned with upholding the dignity of students so that they can undergo the difficulties of liberal education. See his *The Harm in Hate Speech* (Cambridge, MA: Harvard University Press, 2012).
99. The conservative attack on students as snowflakes is really a boldfaced attack of thinking. Students who question our treatment of minorities, marginalized populations, and the ways we talk about them are not scared: they are forcing the powerful to look at injustice, and this makes the powerful afraid and lash out with a label that has, unfortunately, stuck.
100. I think a great example of work that is deeply difficult—asking us to question fundamental assumptions about who we are—but at the same time mindful of leading a reader through the process of thought without attacking them is Marilyn Frye's *Politics of Reality* (Freedom, CA: Crossing Press, 1983). Again, it is wrong to say that thinking must be argumentative or confrontational in order to be transformative, as Frye very clearly demonstrates.
101. For an excellent discussion of this point, see Talbot Brewer, "The Coup That Failed," *Hedgehog Review* 16, no. 2 (2014): 64–83.
102. Doris Santoro, *Demoralized* (Cambridge, MA: Harvard Education Press, 2018).
103. I try to capture some of my gratitude for Baldwin in my essay "Love and Growth: On One Aspect of James Baldwin's Significance for Education," *Teachers College Record* 117, no. 9 (2015): 1–38.
104. For a philosopher, Miller is notably averse to argument. See section 1 of Miller's *Task of Criticism*, especially the essay "Style in Philosophy," for his thinking on why argument is not the whole—or even the heart—of philosophy.
105. William James, *Writings: 1878–1899* (New York: Library of America, 1992), 861.
106. For a very insightful and interesting contemporary discussion of this fact, see Akeel Bilgrami, "The Visibility of Value," *Social Research* 83, no. 4 (2016): 917–43.
107. Here, I see connections between Emerson's idea that self-reliance will bring

us into community with others, but unlike Emerson, Miller doesn't have a divine backstop to offer certainty that this will come to pass. As well, it is worth noting that the idea of the fateful experience of freedom is central to Vincent Colapietro's wonderful book on Miller, *The Fateful Shapes of Human Freedom*.

108. In addition to being influenced by Emerson on this point, I have to think Miller's thinking on community is shaped by Josiah Royce, especially *The Problem of Christianity* (Washington, DC: Catholic University of America Press, 2001).
109. For an excellent example of free thinking attempting to keep pace with scientific advances, see Owen Flanagan, *The Really Hard Problem* (Cambridge, MA: MIT Press, 2007). See, also, Hans Jonas, *The Imperative of Responsibility* (Chicago, IL: University of Chicago Press, 1985).
110. Here I am reminded of the excellent study of education reform in America, David Tyack and Larry Cuban's *Tinkering toward Utopia* (Cambridge, MA: Harvard University Press, 1995).
111. The rise of MOOCs is well-documented; for personalized learning playlists, see https://www.npr.org/2018/11/16/657895964/the-future-of-learning-well-it-s-personal.
112. For a recent example, see Nellie Bowles, "Dark Consensus," *New York Times*, October 26, 2018. Retrieved from https://www.nytimes.com/2018/10/26/style/phones-children-silicon-valley.html.
113. For an example of resistance to this type of technological colonialization, see Nellie Bowles, "Silicon Valley Came to Kansas. That Started a Rebellion," *New York Times*, April 21, 2019. Retrieved from https://www.nytimes.com/2019/04/21/technology/silicon-valley-kansas-schools.html.
114. Sadly, this rarely happens in education. The very things that people advocate for "other people's children" are not pursued for their own. See David Berliner and Gene Glass, *50 Myths and Lies that Threaten America's Public Schools* (New York: Teachers College Press, 2014).
115. In James, *Writings*.
116. It is important that one of the originators of "Visible Thinking" wrote a book called *Intellectual Character*. For an overview of visible thinking, see http://www.pz.harvard.edu/projects/visible-thinking and Karin Morrison, Mark Church, and Ron Ritchhart, *Making Thinking Visible* (San Francisco, CA: Jossey-Bass, 2001).
117. For more on this, see my book review of *Building a Better Teacher*, *Education, and Culture* 31, no. 1 (2015): 89–95.
118. See: Hansen, "Person and Role in Teaching."

119. Saying this, the use of robotic teachers may be more common in the future. For example, see https://www.axios.com/robot-ai-teaching-college-course-at-west-point-98ce5888-873b-4b72-8de5-0f7c592d66b0.html.
120. For a fascinating discussion of covenant, see John Schaar, *Legitimacy and the State* (New Brunswick, NJ: Transaction, 1981), esp. 291 ff. This point is picked up in very interesting ways by Philip Selznick, *The Moral Commonwealth* (Berkeley, CA: University of California Press, 1992), esp. 480 ff.
121. Susan McWilliams makes the very insightful point that noted political thinker Sheldon Wolin's deep commitment to democracy was likely fostered though his experience of liberal education, as embodied by Oberlin College. See her "Teaching Political Theory as Vocation," *The Good Society* 24, no. 2 (2015): 191–97.
122. I feel tremendously lucky that I had Jim Alouf and Holly Gould as colleagues as a new professor at Sweet Briar College. Their devotion to the art of teaching and to their students was deeply educative.
123. This theme runs through most of Dewey's work; it is seen very powerfully in his *Democracy and Education* in *Middle Works of John Dewey, Volume 9* (Carbondale, IL: Southern Illinois University Press, 2008).
124. This policing of thought is not limited to any one type of college: it occurs whenever a teacher does not allow students to experience the transformative power of thinking. For a good, recent discussion of this type of thinking, see Alan Jacobs, *How to Think* (New York: Currency, 2017).
125. For a discussion, see https://www.chronicle.com/article/Sokal-Squared-Is-Huge/244714.
126. Though I use the term *trustee of value* in this book, I think this is a nice parallel between thinking that we should educate doctoral students to see themselves as stewards of the discipline. For a discussion, see Chris Golde and George Walker, *Envisioning the Future of Doctoral Education: Preparing Stewards of the Discipline* (San Francisco, CA: Jossey-Bass, 2006).
127. For a discussion of this point, see Jeff Frank, *Teaching in the Now* (West Lafayette, IN: Purdue University Press, 2018).
128. For any reader who has dreaded committee work, it is hard to imagine we are being permissive by obligating students to do this work.
129. See Arthur Brooks, "Loneliness Is Tearing America Apart," *New York Times*, November 23, 2018. Retrieved from: https://www.nytimes.com/2018/11/23/opinion/loneliness-political-polarization.html.
130. Robert Putnam, *Bowling Alone* (New York: Simon & Schuster, 2001).
131. Here, I appreciate how Michael Oakeshott describes liberal education as a conversation. See his *The Voice of Liberal Learning* (Indianapolis, IN: Liberty Fund, 1989).

132. For a very insightful discussion of why we should not stand in fear of cliché when it comes to liberal education, see Kevin Gary, "The Wisdom of Clichés," *Philosophy of Education Yearbook 2014*. Retrieved from https://educationjournal.web.illinois.edu/archive/index.php/pes/article/view/4890.pdf.
133. For an excellent discussion of related points, see Scheffler, *Equality and Tradition*, especially "The Normativity of Tradition."
134. Here, again, I think of Emerson and Royce's thinking on the great community. I am also reminded of a wonderful line from *Souls of Black Folk*, where Du Bois sees the ends of our striving to be educated as the desire to be "co-workers in the kingdom of culture." W. E. B. Du Bois, *Souls of Black Folk*, in *Writings* (New York: Library of America, 1987), 365.
135. Dewey, *Democracy and Education*, 176.
136. I worry that at times, especially when discussing higher education administration, that I get too defensive. I think the best response to problems around the administration of higher education is to build administrative capacity around the central mission of liberal education. As touched on briefly, book studies about liberal education should be a part of orientation and ongoing professional development at liberal arts colleges.
137. Emerson, *Essays*, 264.
138. On the spiral curriculum, see Jerome Bruner, *Process of Education* (Cambridge, MA: Harvard University Press, 1960).
139. I see this sense of circling as central to Robert Frost's philosophy of education, a topic of my dissertation and touched on briefly in my review of Robert Frost's notebooks for the *Teachers College Record*. Retrieved from: https://www.tcrecord.org/content.asp?contentid=13835
140. For a rich discussion of exemplars in education, see Linda Zagzebski, *Exemplarist Moral Theory* (New York: Oxford, 2017).
141. Emerson, *Essays*, 266.
142. Implicit here is that grading and feedback are not the same thing. For a nice primer on giving effective feedback, though it is geared toward younger students, see Susan Brookhart, *How to Give Effective Feedback to Your Students* (Alexandria, VA: Association for Supervision and Curriculum Development, 2017).
143. For an excellent discussion of this sense of being placeless, see Wendell Berry's work. One can find this theme running throughout his fiction, poems, and essays. For a good starting point, see *Our Only World* (Berkeley, CA: Counterpoint, 2015).
144. Richard Rorty spells out the philosophical implications of contingency clearly and dramatically in his *Contingency, Irony, Solidarity* (New York: Cambridge

University Press, 1989). Though I feel as if I disagree with Rorty's thinking on contingency—I feel an acknowledgement of contingency can still lead to loyalty, not ironic loyalty, but strong loyalty—I don't have time to expand on this point here. One might contrast Rorty's thinking on irony with Bernard Williams's thinking on confidence. For an excellent discussion, see Miranda Fricker, "Confidence and Irony," in *Morality, Reflection, and Ideology* (New York: Oxford University Press, 2000).

145. Here we can think about Josiah Royce's thinking on loyalty and how this influenced Miller's own thinking on local control. See Josiah Royce, *Philosophy of Loyalty* (New York: MacMillan, 1914).
146. Miller, *Midworld*, 191.
147. Miller, *Midworld*, 191.
148. For example, some college campuses make it difficult to do good work. In these cases, one should look for opportunities to teach at places that are supportive of liberal education, even while one also tries to keep the spark of liberal education alive for students.
149. Yascha Mounk, *The People vs. Democracy* (Cambridge, MA: Harvard University Press, 2018).
150. See, for example, Jason Stanley, *How Fascism Works* (New York: Random House, 2018).
151. For an exceptionally strong and interesting discussion of Miller's politics, see Vincent Colapietro, "The Reclamation of History," in *Commonplace Commitments*, eds. Peter S. Fosl, Michael J. McGandy, and Mark D. Moorman (Lewisburg, PA: Bucknell University Press, 2016).
152. See Murray's autobiography *Song in a Weary Throat* (New York: Norton, 1987), esp. chap. 33.
153. To which a defender of campus protest may assert: but the other side is full of hatred and violence, we are fighting for justice. I think we can usefully sidestep this debate altogether by considering what allows for the type of thinking that will build a foundation capable of sustaining the difficulty of liberal education. Populism does not strike me as the foundation from which we should build. For an interesting discussion of related points, see Alan Jacobs, "Wokeness and Myth on Campus," *The New Atlantis* 53 (2017): 33–44.
154. One can see this pressure coming from groups like Reedies Against Racism. For an overview, see "Students Said a Keystone Course Was Racist," in *Chronicle of Higher Education*. See https://www.chronicle.com/article/Students-Said-a-Keystone/243095. Right-wing critiques of liberal education make it appear that these types of protests are normal at liberal colleges, supported and encouraged by faculty, and indicative of their illiberal nature. This is not

true. But explaining why it isn't true is something that college communities should talk about more regularly than they do.

155. For a really excellent discussion of a related point, see Rebecca Hanrahan and Louise Antony, "Because I Said So," *Hypatia* 20, no. 4 (2005): 59–79. Hanrahan and Antony make the important point that a feminist teacher is an authority in the classroom, but this is completely consonant with the teacher's belief in the liberatory power of feminist thinking.

156. I see similarities between this line of thinking in Hannah Arendt's philosophy of education. For an excellent discussion of Arendt's philosophy of education, see the special issue Chris Higgins edited for the *Teachers College Record.* The table of contents can be accessed at https://www.tcrecord.org/Issue.asp?volyear=2010&number=2&volume=112.

157. For an excellent defense of the power of poetry in politically difficult times, see Clare Cavanaugh, *Lyric Poetry and Modern Politics* (New Haven, CT: Yale University Press, 2010).

158. For an excellent discussion of the place of piety in Miller's thinking, see Colapietro, *Fateful Shapes of Human Freedom*.

www.ingramcontent.com/pod-product-compliance
Lightning Source LLC
LaVergne TN
LVHW050023250826
846302LV00009B/69
9781643150079